LEARN TO
knit

LEARN TO
knit

EDITED BY
Sue Whiting

PHOTOGRAPHS BY
John Heseltine

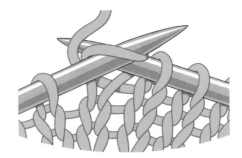

First published in Great Britain 2005 by
Coats Crafts UK
Lingfield Point
McMullen Road
Darlington
Co. Durham DL1 1YQ
UK

First published May 2005
Reprinted August 2005 and January 2006

Editor Sally Harding
Design Anne Wilson
Illustrations Kate Simunek
Photography John Heseltine
Styling Susan Berry

**British Library Cataloguing in Publication
Data**
A catalogue record for this book is available
from the British Library

ISBN 1 904485 31 6

Reproduced and printed in Singapore

Contents

Introduction

When learning to knit, you need to understand how knitting is created and what tools you will need. To make a flat piece of knitting, you work with two needles and a continuous length of yarn, which can be natural fibres, such as wool, cotton or silk, or manmade ones, such as nylon or acrylic. The finished pieces are then stitched together to make a garment or other project. If you want to make a tubular item like socks, without seams, you need to use four double-pointed needles.

The projects in this book are starred in terms of complexity, but none of them is difficult. The introduction to each garment explains those suitable for first-time knitters.

The materials and tools you will need include the yarn and the knitting needles, plus some basic sewing, cutting and measuring equipment. The look of your knitting will be determined to a large extent by the chosen yarn and the types of stitches used. Today, there are many different kinds of yarn available, including all forms of fancy and novelty yarns. In this book, we have chosen standard yarns that knit up well and keep their shape after washing.

Yarns

The character of any yarn is determined by its composition and thickness.

Pure wool This has great insulation: warm in winter and cool in summer. Soft and springy, it is comfortable and absorbent. Treated pure wools are machine washable.

Cotton, linen and silk These create an attractive finish but have little natural elasticity. As a result, they are often combined with other fibres that have these properties. They are comfortable to wear next to the skin but linen and silk are relatively expensive.

Acrylic A manmade fibre, it is lighter than wool and cheaper. It can be machine washed and dries quickly, but lacks the natural springiness and flexibility of wool.

Nylon Also manmade, this fibre also lacks the springiness of wool but is relatively inexpensive.

Blended fibres Most spinners now blend different fibres to produce attractive yarns with textural effects, known as novelty yarns.

Yarn weight and ply Yarn is created from single spun threads or strands which are then twisted together. The ensuing yarn is referred to as 2 ply (2 strands), 3 ply (3 strands) or 4 ply (4 strands). Fine 2-ply or 3-ply yarns take a long time to knit, so 4 ply is nowadays the finest yarn generally used. Double-knitting (DK) yarns are about twice the thickness of 4-ply yarns, and chunky yarns are generally twice as thick as double-knitting, and are ideal for outdoor wear.

Four different yarns are used in this book. From left to right: 4-ply cotton, 4-ply wool, double knitting (DK) wool and chunky wool (see page 79).

Needle types and sizes

Knitting needles come in a range of sizes, from very fine to really fat (see list opposite). A range of materials are used for them, including steel, plastic and, most recently, bamboo (as shown below). It is important to choose needles that feel comfortable in your hands, and that allow the stitches to slide along easily.

The type of yarn and style of pattern will determine the needle size you use.

Generally, most garments require an average-size needle. The edges on a garment are often knitted in a rib stitch on a size smaller needle than the main body, as this gives the ribbing extra elasticity.

If you are knitting seamless garments, you will need to use four needles, rather than two (see page 13). Garments with more stitches than usual may require a special circular needle (see below centre).

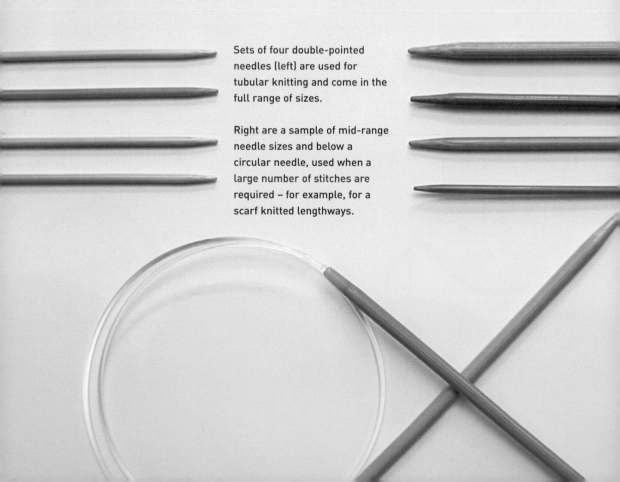

Sets of four double-pointed needles (left) are used for tubular knitting and come in the full range of sizes.

Right are a sample of mid-range needle sizes and below a circular needle, used when a large number of stitches are required – for example, for a scarf knitted lengthways.

Tension

Comparative needle sizes

EU METRIC	OLD UK	UK METRIC	US
2mm	14	2mm	0
	13	2¼mm	1
2½mm			
	12	2¾mm	2
3mm	11	3mm	
	10	3¼mm	3
3½mm	9	3¾mm	5
4mm	8	4mm	
			6
4½mm	7	4½mm	7
5mm	6	5mm	8
5½mm	5	5½mm	9
6mm	4	6mm	10
6½mm	3	6½mm	10½
7mm	2	7mm	
7½mm	1	7½mm	
8mm	0	8mm	11
9mm	00	9mm	13
10mm	000	10mm	15

To make a successful hand-knitted garment to the chosen size, it is essential that you work to the stated tension – the correct number of stitches and rows over a 10cm (4in) square. To check that your own tension is the same as that of the pattern, you need to make a small sample square approximately 12cm (5in) in size BEFORE you start to knit a pattern. You then smooth out the sample square, taking care not to stretch the fabric, and count the stitches and rows to 10cm (4in).

If there are fewer rows and stitches to 10cm (4in) than those specified in your pattern, your own tension is too loose, and you therefore need to use a size smaller needle. If you have too many stitches and rows, your tension is too tight, and a size larger needle will be needed.

Notes for patterns

The patterns in this book are graded as easy (✪), intermediate (✪✪) and advanced (✪✪✪). Novice knitters should start with those marked ✪.

Abbreviations generally used in all patterns are given on page 78.

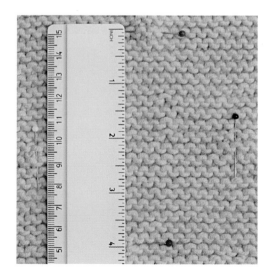

Casting on

To make the very first loops on your needles, you 'cast on' stitches. There are several methods, but all of them require you, in the first place, to create an initial loop on your needle. A commonly used technique is shown here. All cast-on loops should be made as evenly as possible. Avoid casting on too tightly. The cast-on stitches should slide freely on the needle.

MAKING THE FIRST LOOP

1 Wrap the yarn around the first and second fingers of one hand.

2 Place the tip of the needle under the front loop and draw the back loop through the front one.

3 Withdraw your fingers from the loop, then tighten it on the needle to form the first stitch.

1

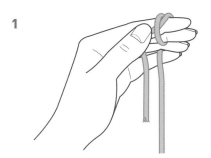

2

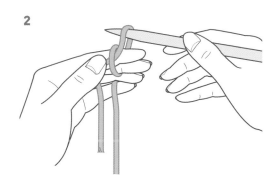

3

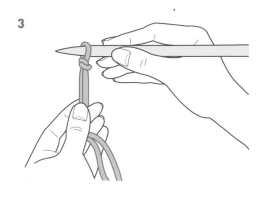

THUMB CAST-ON

This is a common, and easy, method of casting on. The tail end of the yarn is held in the right hand and the ball end of the yarn (also called the working yarn) is held in the left hand.

1 With the initial loop on the needle, held in the right hand, hold the working yarn in the palm of the left hand, as shown, passing it around the thumb. If necessary to keep the loop on the needle in place, hold the tail end of the yarn with the right hand. Pass the tip of the needle from front to back under the front strand of yarn on the thumb as shown by the arrow.

2 With the strand of yarn around your thumb caught by the needle, gently slip your left thumb out of the loop.

3 Tighten the new loop on the needle, but make sure it will still glide along the needle. You have now made the second cast-on loop.

4 Reinsert your left thumb under the working yarn to begin the next cast-on loop. Continue to cast on stiches by repeating steps 1 through 3.

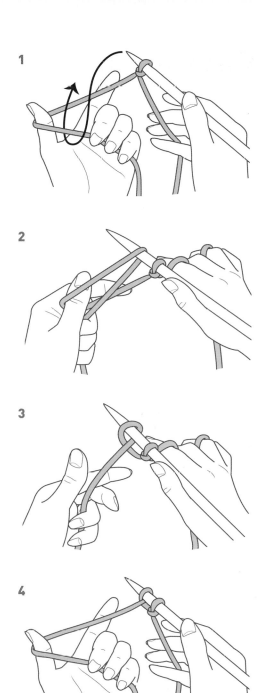

CHAIN-EDGE CAST-ON

This cast-on method gives a looser edge than the thumb cast-on, although it can be tightened to create a firmer, more elastic edge by knitting into the back of the stitches on the next row. (If you are a complete beginner, turn to pages 14 and 15 before you try this cast-on to find out how to hold the needles and yarn.)

1 Make a starting loop on the needle as already described (see page 10) and hold this needle in your left hand. Hold the ball end of the yarn and the other needle in your right hand. Insert the right needle through the loop as shown and pass the yarn around the tip.

2 With the tip of the right needle, pull the yarn through the loop on the left needle to create a new loop on the right needle.

3 Transfer this new loop onto the left needle, by inserting the tip of the left needle from right to left through the front of the loop. Withdraw the right needle, then reinsert it through the loop just made, as shown, to start the next cast-on stitch. Repeat steps 1 through 3 to cast on as many stitches as you need.

1

2
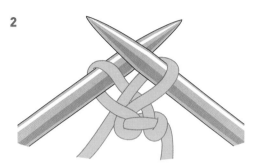

3

Working with four needles

When you want to knit a tube, without a seam, you use four needles rather than two. When you knit, you simply work clockwise around three needles, using the fourth as the working needle. First, of course, you have to cast on stitches onto three of the four needles. A chain-edge cast-on is recommended.

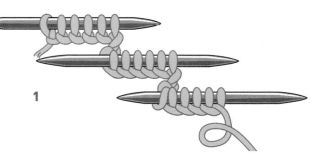

1

Cast on with four needles

1 Using the chain-edge cast-on, cast on the stitches onto one needle, then divide them evenly between the three needles.

2 To start to knit, arrange the three needles in a triangle. The working yarn will be at the end of the third needle.

3 Loosely knot a coloured thread around the needle next to the working yarn to mark the start of the rounds. Then start to knit with the fourth needle, closing the cast-on triangle when knitting through the first stitch on the first needle.

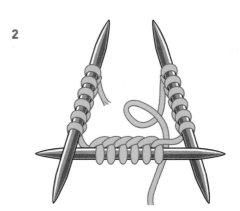

2

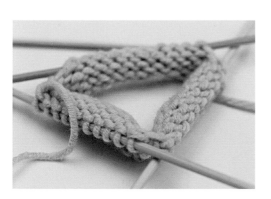

3

Knitting basics

There are only two basic stitches in knitting: knit and purl. All knitted fabrics are made using combinations, or variations, of these stitches.

   To begin, you need to learn how to hold your needles and yarn. Most garments are knitted with two needles (see page 13 to create tubular knitting with four needles). If you are right handed, hold the needle with the existing stitches in your left hand and the working needle and yarn in your right hand. Most people thread the yarn through the right hand, with the ball end of the yarn

around the little finger, under the third and fourth fingers, and over the forefinger, which controls the movement of the yarn.

Continental knitting

A different method of holding the yarn, known as Continental knitting, is preferred by some. With practice, it can make knitting quicker. In it, the left hand controls the yarn and the right hand controls the needle. The hands are held over the top of the work, and the left needle is held between the thumb and second finger, leaving the left hand index finger free to work the yarn, which is looped around the finger.

How to work the knit stitch
1 Keeping the yarn at the back of the work, insert the tip of the right needle into the front of the first stitch on the left needle. Grab the working yarn with the tip of the right needle and pull it through to the front.

2 Allow the stitch on the left needle to slip off, leaving a new stitch on the right needle. Continue in this way to the end of the row. Then turn to start the next row.

How to work the purl stitch
3 Keeping the working yarn at the front of the work, insert the right needle from right to left through the front of the first stitch on the left needle.

4 Take the yarn over and around the needle, then pull it through to the back of the work, controlling the work as shown. Slip the old stitch off the left needle, leaving a new stitch on the right needle. Continue in this way.

1

2

3

4
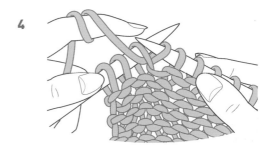

Knit stitch

This is the first stitch you learn and is abbreviated in knitting patterns as k. It creates a simple ridged fabric known as garter stitch when worked on its own. When worked in alternate rows with purl stitch (opposite), it forms a smooth textured stitch known as stocking stitch (right). Knit stitches

Stocking stitch is created by working knit and purl rows alternately. The knit side is the right side.

are formed by inserting the tip of the knitting needle through from front to back of each stitch, passing the yarn around the needle and drawing a loop through.

1

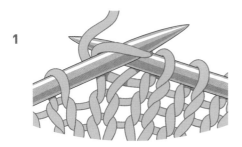

How to work the knit stitch
1 Insert the tip of the right needle through the first loop on the left needle, from front to back. Then wrap the working yarn around the tip of the right needle.

2

2 Pull the tip of the right needle and the yarn through the loop on the left needle.

3

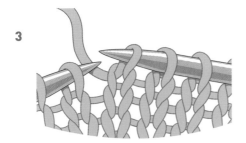

3 Slip the old loop off the left needle to complete the stitch. Continue knitting stitches in this way until all the stitches on the left needle have been knitted onto the right needle. You have now completed one row of the knit stitch.

Purl stitch

This is the second stitch to learn and is very similar to the knit stitch. If all rows are purled a garter stitch fabric is created. When purl rows are combined alternately with knit rows, they form stocking stitch. The purl side of the stocking stitch fabric is called reverse stocking stitch. When a purl stitch is worked

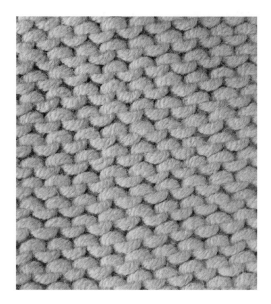

Reverse stocking stitch is worked in the same way as stocking stitch. The right side is the purl side.

the yarn is held at the front of the work rather than at the back of the work as with the knit stitch.

1

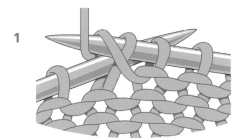

2

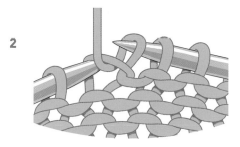

3

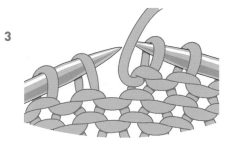

How to work the purl stitch

1 Insert the right needle through the front of the first stitch on the left needle from right to left and wrap the working yarn around the tip of the needle as shown.

2 With the tip of the right needle, pull the yarn through the loop on the left needle.

3 Slip the old loop off the left needle, leaving a new stitch on the right needle. This completes the purl stitch. Continue in the same way until all the stitches on the left needle have been purled. This completes one purl row.

Shaping

You shape your knitting by adding or subtracting stitches from the rows, as you work. There are various methods of adding and subtracting stitches to create different styles and effects.

Increasing

The first two increasing techniques given below are usually used near the edges of the knitting for side shaping. All the increases are shown worked on a knit row, but the same simple principles can be applied to a purl row.

SIMPLE INCREASE

Knit into the front of the stitch in the usual way. But before slipping the old stitch off the needle, knit into the back of the stitch, forming two stitches on the right needle.

MAKING A STITCH

This method is different from a simple increase in that it does not use an existing stitch to make another stitch. It is abbreviated as M1 in patterns. Pick up the horizontal loop between two stitches and work into the back of it to make a stitch, as shown. To make two stitches, referred to as M2 in patterns, work into the front of the loop after first working into the back of it.

INVISIBLE INCREASE

This is ideal for increasing in the middle of a row as it is virtually invisible. Insert the tip of the right needle into the front of the stitch below the next stitch to be knitted and knit it.

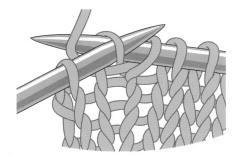

Simple increase

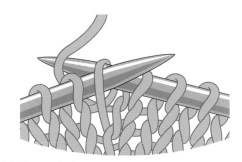

Making a stitch

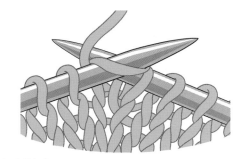

Invisible increase

Decreasing

Decreases are made by working two stitches as one. The joined loops of knitting slope either to the right or left depending on the technique used. If used for decorative purposes, decreases are carefully chosen to create the right detail.

SIMPLE KNIT DECREASE (RIGHT)

This forms a decrease that slopes to the right. Knit two stitches together by inserting the tip of the right needle through the next two stitches instead of one, and knitting these together as one stitch. This is called k2tog.

SIMPLE KNIT DECREASE (LEFT)

This forms a decrease that slopes to the left. Knit two stitches together but insert the tip of the right needle through the back of the stitches. This is called k2tog tbl.

ALTERNATIVE KNIT DECREASE (LEFT)

This also forms a decrease that slopes to the left. Slip one stitch knitways onto the right needle without knitting it, knit the next stitch, then pass the slipped stitch over the knit stitch and off the right needle.

SIMPLE PURL DECREASE (RIGHT)

This forms a right slope on the knit side of the fabric. Insert the needle purlways through two stitches and purl them together as one stitch – called p2tog.

Although the knit decreases shown above can be adapted to create purl decreases (by simply purling instead of knitting the stitches) both increases and decreases are usually worked on the knit rows where possible, except for intricate stitch textures or knitted lace.

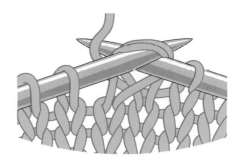

Simple knit decrease (sloping right)

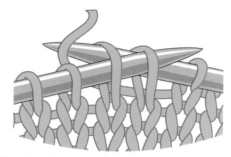

Simple knit decrease (sloping left)

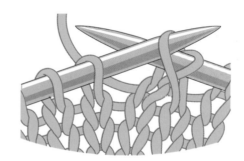

Alternative knit decrease (sloping left)

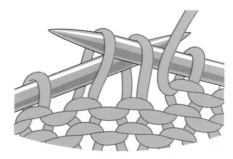

Simple purl decrease (sloping right)

Casting off

The finished cast-off edge.

Once you have completed your knitting, you will need to finish off the work. This is known as casting off. The stitches can be cast off as they are knitted, purled or worked in a pattern stitch, but the method is the same. The simple knit cast-off is shown below.

1

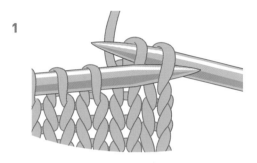

2

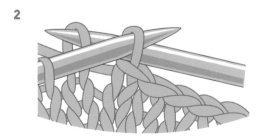

3

How to cast off

Be careful when casting off not to do so too tightly. You can use a size larger needle to avoid this, if you wish.

1 Knit the first two stitches. Then pick up the first stitch with the tip of the left needle and pass it over the second stitch and off the right needle all together, to leave one stitch on the right handle.

2 Now knit the next stitch so there are two stitches again on the right needle. Cast off another stitch by repeating step 1.

3 Continue to cast off stitch by stitch across the row until only one stitch remains. Break the yarn, draw the end through the last stitch, and slip the stitch off the needle. Pull the yarn to fasten off. The tail end will be darned in later during making up.

Finishing touches

There are a number of useful tips and techniques that will help ensure a professional finish on your garment.

Blocking
When you have finished the various parts of the garment, they should be pressed. Check the ball band for any pressing instructions. Pin out each piece of knitted fabric, wrong side uppermost, on an ironing sheet and check the measurements against the pattern instructions. Then block out each piece by pinning around the edges, to the size required. Lightly press in place, with a clean, damp cloth between the iron and the knitting. Avoid pressing the ribbing as this lessens its elasticity.

Seams
The majority of garments are made up with a backstitch seam, which gives a tailored finish. For baby garments and delicate fabrics, use a flat seam. For ribbing, use invisible seams.

BACKSTITCH SEAM
Place the two pieces of fabric right sides together, and pin in position. Sew together with a row of backstitches, worked one stitch in from the edge, as shown.

FLAT SEAM
Place the two pieces of fabric right sides together, and pin in position. Sew together with loose oversewing stitches, matching ridge to ridge.

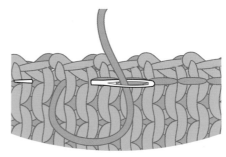
Backstitch seam

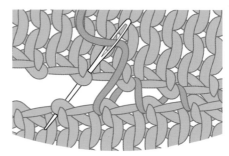
Flat seam

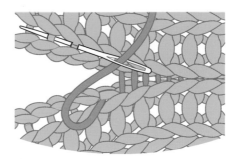
Invisible seam

INVISIBLE SEAM
With the right sides of the knitting facing you, place the two pieces of fabric side by side. Stitch together as shown, working one stitch from each edge in turn, as shown.

Buttonholes and buttonbands

If your garment has separately worked button and buttonhole bands, you should first pin the fronts to the back at shoulder seams. Then pin the bands to the front, taking care to ensure that the lower edge of the garment forms a straight edge. One stitch should be taken from the band and the cardigan to form the seam.

REINFORCED CARDIGAN BANDS

You can create a really professional finish on a cardigan by reinforcing the front bands with grosgrain-ribbon facings. First, pin a facing in place on the wrong side of each band, taking care not to stretch the knitting. Slipstitch the facings in place, as shown. On the buttonhole band, cut the buttonholes in the facing to match the buttonholes on the garment and work buttonhole stitch around each one using a matching sewing thread. Sew the buttons to the button band in corresponding positions.

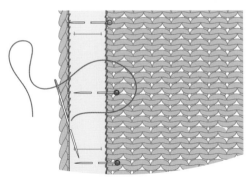

Positioning buttonband facing

BUTTONHOLES

To knit a horizontal buttonhole, work to the position of the buttonhole, bind off one, two or three stitches, then work to the end of the row. On the next row, cast on the same number of stitches over those cast-off. On the following row, pick up the loose thread at the base of the buttonhole, work the next stitch and pass the picked up stitch over it.

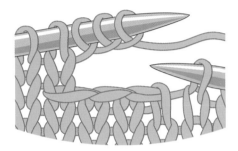

Horizontal buttonhole

To make a vertical buttonhole, divide the stitches at the buttonhole position and work an equal number of rows on each set of stitches, then join up with a row of stitches worked right across.

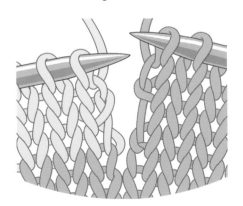

Vertical buttonhole

Neckbands

When you work the neck trimming on a garment, you will usually have to pick up stitches along the edge of the knitting. The following tips help to create a tidy edging.

On a V-neck sweater, a neat appearance is achieved by keeping a single knit stitch up the centre front, on the right side of the work. To do this, pick up an even number of stitches on each side of the V and one at the centre front, so when you work in k1, p1 rib, this centre stitch will always be a k1. The V is shaped by working a decrease on each side of the centre k1.

It is easiest to pick up stitches evenly if you divide the edge with pins. If you have 60 stitches to pick up, for example, along the front slope off a cardigan, you can divide this into 10 equal sections with pins and pick up six stitches in each section.

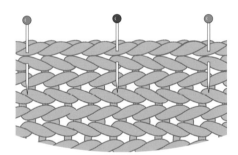

Dividing the neck evenly

Picking up and knitting stitches

When you pick up and knit along cast-off stitches across the front and back of the neck, knit through both loops. This will avoid loose stitches and ladder-like holes.

A shaped edge where decreases have been worked has an alternate long and short stitch. Knit through all loops as required, spacing them evenly, but work twice into long loops for more stitches or omit some of

the long loops for less. When picking up and knitting stitches along the straight side of the neck (through rows), insert the needle through both loops.

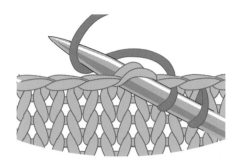

Picking up stitches along cast-off stitches

Picking up dropped stitches

If a stitch is accidentally dropped, it is easiest to use a crochet hook to pick it up, even if it has unravelled a few rows down. To pick up knit stitches, insert the hook into the dropped stitch, catch the bar lying above the dropped stitch and pull it through. To pick up purl stitches, simply turn the work over and use the same method as for knit stitches.

Joining in new yarn

Whenever possible, join a new ball of yarn at the beginning of a row. Where a new ball of yarn has to be joined in the middle of a row, you can make a neat join by splicing the yarn. Unravel a short length of the yarn from the old ball and the new one, and cut away a strand or two from each. Twist the remaining strands together to make one thickness of yarn. Knit carefully through this join, trimming off any stray ends.

gallery of projects

Pot holder

⭐ *This little pot holder is worked in three colours, and forms a pocket to insert your hand. The colourwork pattern is created by slipping stitches and using only one colour in each row. Slipstitch colourwork patterns form a dense fabric that is perfect for pot holders.*

You will need
- *Patons Diploma Gold DK*:
  - 1 x 50g ball in **MS** – dark blue (shade no. 6169)
  - Small amount in each of **1st C** – light olive green (shade no. 6253); and **2nd C** – denim blue (shade no. 6136)
- Pair of 3¼mm (US 3) knitting needles
- 2cm (¾in) diameter curtain ring

Tension and finished size
- 22 stitches and 38 rows to 10cm (4in) over pattern using 3¼mm (US 3) needles.
- Pot holder measures 20.5cm (8in) square.

Main section (make 2)
With 3¼mm (US 3) needles and MS, cast on 43 sts.
Starting with a k row, work in stocking st for 2 rows, ending with RS facing for next row.
Join in 1st C and **patt** thus:
Row 1 (RS) Using 1st C, k1, *sl 1 purlways, k3; rep from * to last 2 sts, sl 1 purlways, k1.
Row 2 Using 1st C, k1, bring yarn to front (WS) of work, *sl 1 purlways, p3; rep from * to last 2 sts, sl 1 purlways, k1.
Join in 2nd C.
Row 3 Using 2nd C, k3, *sl 1 purlways, k3; rep from * to end.

Row 4 Using 2nd C, k1, p2, *sl 1 purlways, p3; rep from * to last 4 sts, sl 1 purlways, p2, k1.
Rows 5 and 6 As rows 1 and 2 but using MS.
Rows 7 and 8 As rows 3 and 4 but using 1st C.
Rows 9 and 10 As rows 1 and 2 but using 2nd C.
Rows 11 and 12 As rows 3 and 4 but using MS.
These 12 rows form patt.
Rep rows 1 to 12, 4 times more.
Break off 1st and 2nd C and cont using MS only.

SHAPE END BORDER
Place marker at beg of last row.
Next row (RS) *K2, k2tog tbl; rep from * to last 3 sts, k3 (33 sts).
Work in garter st for 5 rows, inc 1 st at each end of next and foll 2 alt rows (39 sts). Cast off.

Side border
With RS facing, 3¼mm (US 3) needles and MS, **knit up** 31 sts down row-end edge of one piece, from marker to cast-on edge.
Work in garter st for 5 rows, inc 1 st at each end of next and foll 2 alt rows (37 sts). Cast off.
Work one side border on other piece in same way. (Each piece has borders along two sides.)

Make up
Press following instructions on ball band.
Lay pieces WS facing so that there is a border all around holder and join shaped row-end edges of Borders. Neatly slip stitch cast-on and row-end edges in place, leaving one cast-on edge open.
Using MS, work buttonhole st over curtain ring and attach to a top corner.

Cushion cover

✪ *This elegant black, white and grey rectangular cushion looks good in both traditional and contemporary settings. Combine it with other monochrome cushions for a cool urban look, or put it with bright, strong plain colours so that it creates a focal point on a sofa or bed. The slipstitch colourwork is easy to knit because only one colour is used in a row.*

You will need
- *Patons Diploma Gold DK*:
  - 3 x 50g balls in **MS** – black (shade no. 06183)
  - 2 x 50g balls in each of **1st C** – grey (shade no. 06184); and **2nd C** – cream (shade no. 06142)
- Pair each of 3³/4mm (US 5) and 4mm (US 6) knitting needles
- 36cm x 48cm (14in x 19in) cushion pad

Tension and finished size
- 22 stitches and 30 rows to 10cm (4in) over stocking stitch using 4mm (US 6) needles.
- Completed cushion cover measures 36cm x 48cm (14in x 19in).

Special abbreviations
sL2 = slip next 2 sts purlways.
wyib = with yarn in back (WS) of work.
wyif = with yarn in front (WS) of work.

Sides (make 2)
With 3³/4mm (US 5) needles and MS, cast on 76 sts.
Work in garter st for 2 rows, ending with RS facing for next row.

Joining in and breaking off colours as required, **patt** thus:
Change to 4mm (US 6) needles.
Row 1 (RS) Using 1st C, *k4, sL2 wyib; rep from * to last 4 sts, k4.
Row 2 Using 1st C, *p4, sL2 wyif; rep from * to last 4 sts, p4.
Rows 3 and 4 As rows 1 and 2.
Rows 5 and 6 Using MS, knit.
Join in 2nd C.
Row 7 Using 2nd C, k1, *sL2 wyib, k4; rep from * to last 3 sts, sL2 wyib, k1.
Row 8 Using 2nd C, p1, *sL2 wyif, p4; rep from * to last 3 sts, sL2 wyif, p1.
Rows 9 and 10 As rows 7 and 8.
Rows 11 and 12 Using MS, knit.
Rows 13 to 24 As rows 1 to 12.
Rows 25 to 28 As rows 1 to 4.
Change to 3³/4mm (US 5) needles.
Rows 29 to 48 Using MS, knit.
These 48 rows form patt.
Rep rows 1 to 48, twice more, then rows 1 to 28 once more, ending with RS facing for next row.
Cast off.

Make up
Press following instructions on ball band. Join Sides along three edges. Insert cushion pad, then close 4th side.

Tea cosy

✪✪ *The choice of colours for this retro-style tea cosy will give it its appeal. You can opt for interesting combinations, such as the lavender and lime chosen here.*

You will need
- *Patons Diploma Gold DK*:
    1 x 50g ball in **MS** – lavender (shade no. 06242)
    1 x 50g ball in **C** – lime green (shade no. 06125)
- Pair of 4¹/₂mm (US 7) knitting needles

Tension and finished size
- Based on a stocking stitch tension of 21 stitches and 28 rows to 10cm (4in) using 4¹/₂mm (US 7) needles.
- Tea cosy to fit a standard size teapot.

Special note
The pleats of the tea cosy are formed by the yarn not in use being stranded quite tightly across WS of work. When working WS rows, remember to take the yarn to the front (WS) of the work before changing colours. Twist yarns together at the back of the work where necessary to prevent holes from forming.

First side
With 4¹/₂mm (US 7) needles and MS, cast on 56 sts.
Work in garter st for 4 rows, ending with RS facing for next row.
**Join in C.
Patt thus:
Row 1 (RS) Using MS k1, *using C k6, using MS k6; rep from * to last 7 sts, using C k6, using MS k1.
Rows 2 to 6 As row 1.
Rows 7 to 12 Using MS k7, *using C k6, using MS k6; rep from * to last st, using MS k1.
Row 13 and 14 As row 1.
Last 2 rows form patt for rest of Side.
Cont in patt for a further 26 rows, ending with RS facing for next row.
SHAPE TOP
Row 1 (RS) Using MS k1, *using C k2tog, k2, k2tog, using MS k2tog, k2, k2tog; rep from * to last 7 sts, using C k2tog, k2, k2tog, using MS k1 (38 sts).
Row 2 Using MS k1, *using C k4, using MS k4; rep from * to last 5 sts, using C k4, using MS k1.
Row 3 Using MS k1, *using C (k2tog) twice, using MS (k2tog) twice; rep from * to last 5 sts, using C (k2tog) twice, using MS k1 (20 sts).
Row 4 Using MS k1, *using C k2, using MS k2; rep from * to last 3 sts, using C k2, using MS k1.
Row 5 Using MS k1, *using C k2tog, using MS k2tog; rep from * to last 3 sts, using C k2tog, using MS k1 (11 sts).
Row 6 Using MS k1, *using C k1, using MS k1; rep from * to end.**
Break off C and cont using MS **only**.
Row 7 K1, * M1 (by picking up horizontal loop lying before next st and knitting into back of it), k into front and back of next st to inc 1; rep from * to last st, M1, k1 (30 sts).
Break yarn and leave these 30 sts on a holder.

Second side

With 4¹/2mm (US 7) needles and MS, cast on 56 sts.

Work in garter st for 4 rows, ending with RS facing for next row.

Cont as for First Side from ** to **, using C in place of MS and MS in place of C.

Break off C and cont using MS **only**.

Row 7 K1, * M1, k into front and back of next st to inc 1; rep from * to last st, M1, k1 (30 sts).

Do NOT break yarn but leave these 30 sts on a holder.

Make up

Do NOT press.

TOP FRILL

With **WS** facing, 4¹/2mm (US 7) needles and MS, k30 from second side, then 30 from first side (60 sts).

Work in garter st for 9 rows, ending with **WS** facing for next row. Cast off.

Join Sides along row-end edges, leaving openings for handle and spout. Using 2 strands each of MS and C, make a twisted cord approx 30cm (12in) long and knot ends, forming tiny tassels. Thread cord through last two-colour row of Sides, pull up tight and tie in a bow.

The colours are carried across the back of the work, and pulled tight enough to form 'pleats' on the front. For other stranded colourwork, take care NOT to pull the yarns so tight!

Baby slipover

✪✪ *This little slipover is just right for a gift for a newborn baby. Make it and the bootees (see page 38), if you wish, as a matching set. As there is no cable needle involved, working the simple cable is easier than it looks – two stitches are simply twisted around each other on every sixth row of the pattern.*

You will need
- *Patons 100% Cotton 4 ply*:
    1 [**1**] x 100g ball in pink (shade no. 01715)
- Pair each of 2³/₄mm (US 2) and 3¹/₄mm (US 3) knitting needles

Tension and finished size
- 35 stitches and 36 rows to 10cm (4in) over pattern using 3¹/₄mm (US 3) needles.
- To fit a newborn [**0-3 months**] baby, chest 36 [**41**]cm (14 [**16**]in).
- Actual chest measurement – 38 [**42**]cm (15 [**16¹/₂**]in).
- Finished length – 20 [**23**]cm (8 [**9**]in)

Back
With 2³/₄mm (US 2) needles, cast on 59 [**65**] sts.
Rib row 1 (RS) K1, *p1, k1; rep from * to end.
Rib row 2 P1, *k1, p1; rep from * to end.
These 2 rows form rib.
Cont in rib for 2cm (³/₄in), ending with **WS** facing for next row.
To prepare for twisted-stitch cable patt, inc sts on next row thus:
Next row (WS) Rib 2 [**4**], *M1 (by picking up horizontal loop lying before next st and knitting into back of it), rib 9 [**8**]; rep from *

to last 3 [**5**] sts, M1, rib 3 [**5**] (66 [**73**] sts).
Change to 3¹/₄mm (US 3) needles and patt thus:
Row 1 (RS) P2 [**3**], *k2, p3; rep from * to last 4 [**5**] sts, k2, p2 [**3**].
Row 2 K2 [**3**], *p2, k3; rep from * to last 4 [**5**] sts, p2, k2 [**3**].
Rows 3 and 4 As rows 1 and 2.
Row 5 P2 [**3**], *k into front of second st on left needle, then k into front of first st and slip both sts off needle together, p3; rep from * to last 4 [**5**] sts, k into front of second st on left needle, then k into front of first st and slip both sts off needle together, p2 [**3**].
Row 6 As row 2.
These 6 rows form patt.
Cont in patt until Back measures 10 [**11**]cm (4 [**4¹/₂**]in), ending with RS facing for next row.
SHAPE ARMHOLES
Keeping patt correct, cast off 2 sts at beg of next 2 rows (62 [**69**] sts).
Dec 1 st at each end of next 5 rows, then on foll 2 [**3**] alt rows (48 [**53**] sts).**
Cont straight until armhole meas 10 [**12**]cm (4 [**4¹/₂**]in), ending with RS facing for next row.
SHAPE SHOULDERS
Cast off 3 [**4**] sts at beg of next 4 rows, then 4 [**3**] sts at beg of foll 2 rows.
Leave rem 28 [**31**] sts on a holder.

Front
Work as for Back to **.
Work 1 row, ending with RS facing for next row.

Next row (RS) Patt 16 [**17**] sts, work 2 tog, turn and work this side first.

Keeping patt correct, dec 1 st at neck edge on next 7 rows, ending with RS facing for next row (10 [**11**] sts).

Cont straight until Front matches Back to start of shoulder shaping, ending with RS facing for next row.

SHAPE SHOULDER

Cast off 3 [**4**] sts at beg of next and foll alt row. Work 1 row.

Cast off rem 4 [**3**] sts.

With RS facing, slip centre 12 [**15**] sts onto a holder, rejoin yarn to rem sts, work 2 tog, patt to end (17 [**18**] sts).

Complete to match first side, reversing shapings, working an extra row before start of shoulder shaping.

Make up

Press following instructions on ball band.
Join right shoulder seam.

Neck border

With RS facing and 2³/4mm (US 2) needles, **knit up** 27 [**34**] sts down left side of neck, k12 [**15**] from front, **knit up** 27 [**34**] sts up right side of neck, then k28 [**31**] from back dec 1 st at centre (93 [**113**] sts).

Starting with rib row 2, work in rib as for Back for 5 rows, ending with RS facing for next row.

Cast off in rib.

Join left shoulder and Neck Border seam.

Armhole borders (both alike)

With RS facing and 2³/4mm (US 2) needles, **knit up** 67 [**73**] sts all round armhole edge.

Starting with rib row 2, work in rib as for Back for 5 rows, ending with RS facing for next row.

Cast off in rib.

Join side and Armhole Border seams.

Cot blanket

✪✪ *This leaf-motif cot blanket is fun to work, and will suit more experienced knitters who want to try their hand at an interesting pattern. You make the motifs first, then join them.*

You will need
- *Patons Diploma Gold DK*:
    7 x 50g balls in green (shade no. 06125)
- Pair each of 3¼mm (US 3) and 4mm (US 6) knitting needles

Tension and finished size
- One motif measures 8cm (3in) square using 4mm (US 6) needles.
- Blanket measures 54cm x 70cm (21½in x 27½in).

Motif (make 48)
With 4mm (US 6) needles, cast on 3 sts.
Row 1 (RS) K3.
Row 2 K1, p1, k1.
Row 3 Inc in first st, k1, inc in last st (5 sts).
Row 4 Inc in first st, k1, p1, k1, inc in last st (7 sts).
Row 5 Inc in first st, p1, k3, p1, inc in last st (9 sts).
Row 6 K3, p3, k3.
Row 7 K2, p1, (k1, yfwd) twice, k1, p1, k2 (11 sts).
Row 8 K3, p5, k3.
Row 9 K2, p1, k2, yfwd, k1, yfwd, k2, p1, k2 (13 sts).
Row 10 K2, inc in next st, p7, inc in next st, k2 (15 sts).
Row 11 K2, p2, k3, yfwd, k1, yfwd, k3, p2, k2 (17 sts).

Row 12 K4, p9, k4.
Row 13 K2, p2, k4, yfwd, k1, yfwd, k4, p2, k2 (19 sts).
Row 14 K3, inc in next st, p11, inc in next st, k3 (21 sts).
Row 15 K2, p3, k5, yfwd, k1, yfwd, k5, p3, k2 (23 sts).
Row 16 K5, p13, k5.
Row 17 K2, p3, k6, yfwd, k1, yfwd, k6, p3, k2 (25 sts).
Row 18 K4, inc in next st, p15, inc in next st, k4 (27 sts).
Row 19 K1, inc in next st, p4, k7, yfwd, k1, yfwd, k7, p4, inc in next st, k1 (31 sts).
Row 20 K7, p17, k7.
Row 21 K1, k2tog, p4, k7, sL1K, k2tog, psso, k7, p4, k2tog, k1 (27 sts).
Row 22 K4, k2tog, p15, k2tog, k4 (25 sts).
Row 23 K2, p3, k6, sL1K, k2tog, psso, k6, p3, k2 (23 sts).
Row 24 As row 16.
Row 25 K2, p3, k5, sL1K, k2tog, psso, k5, p3, k2 (21 sts).
Row 26 K3, k2tog, p11, k2tog, k3 (19 sts).
Row 27 K2, p2, k4, sL1K, k2tog, psso, k4, p2, k2 (17 sts).
Row 28 As row 12.
Row 29 K2, p2, k3, sL1K, k2tog, psso, k3, p2, k2 (15 sts).
Row 30 K2, k2tog, p7, k2tog, k2 (13 sts).
Row 31 K2, p1, k2, sL1K, k2tog, psso, k2, p1, k2 (11 sts).
Row 32 As row 8.
Row 33 K2, p1, k1, sL1K, k2tog, psso, k1, p1, k2 (9 sts).
Row 34 As row 6.

Row 35 K2, p1, sL1K, k2tog, psso, p1, k2
(7 sts).
Row 36 K1, k2tog, p1, k2tog, k1 (5 sts).
Row 37 K2tog, k1, k2tog (3 sts).
Row 38 K3tog and fasten off.

Make up

Press following instructions on ball band, pressing each Motif to 8cm (3in) square. Stitch four Motifs tog to form a square with 'leaf stems' at centre. Join 11 more sets of four Motifs in this way. Then join squares to form a rectangle six Motifs wide and eight Motifs long.

Border

With 3¹/₄mm (US 3) needles, cast on 7 sts.
Row 1 (RS) K7.
Row 2 K3, p1, k3.
Row 3 K2, p1, inc twice in next st, p1, k2
(9 sts).
Row 4 K3, p3, k3.
Row 5 K2, p1, (k1, yfwd) twice, k1, p1, k2
(11 sts).
Row 6 K3, p5, k3.
Row 7 K2, p1, k2, yfwd, k1, yfwd, k2, p1, k2
(13 sts).
Row 8 K3, p7, k3.
Row 9 K2, p1, k3, yfwd, k1, yfwd, k3, p1, k2
(15 sts).
Row 10 K3, p9, k3.
Row 11 K2, p1, k3, sL1K, k2tog, psso, k3, p1,
k2 (13 sts).
Row 12 As row 8.
Row 13 K2, p1, k2, sL1K, k2tog, psso, k2, p1,
k2 (11 sts).
Row 14 As row 6.
Row 15 K2, p1, k1, sL1K, k2tog, psso, k1, p1,
k2 (9 sts).
Row 16 As row 4.
Row 17 K2, p1, sL1K, k2tog, psso, p1, k2
(7 sts).

Row 18 As row 2.
Rows 19 to 22 K7.
These 22 rows form patt.
Rep last 22 rows 7 times more, then rows 1 to 18 again, ending with RS facing for next row.

TURN CORNER
Row 1 (RS) K5, turn.
Row 2 K5.
Row 3 K3, turn.
Row 4 K3.
Rows 5 and 6 K7.
Rows 7 to 12 As rows 1 to 6.
Rows 13 to 16 As rows 1 to 4.
These 16 rows complete corner.
Now work patt rows 1 to 22, 11 times, then rows 1 to 18 again, ending with RS facing for next row.
Work corner turning rows 1 to 16 once more.
Now work patt rows 1 to 22, 8 times, then rows 1 to 18 again, ending with RS facing for next row.
Work corner turning rows 1 to 16 once more.
Now work patt rows 1 to 22, 11 times, then rows 1 to 18 again, ending with RS facing for next row.
Work corner turning rows 1 to 16 once more.
Cast off.
Join cast-on and cast-off ends of Border.
Sew Border to outer edges of joined Motifs.

Baby slippers

✪ *Knitted in cool 100 per cent cotton, these are the perfect gift for a newborn baby. They will take only an evening or two at most to knit.*

You will need
- *Patons 100% Cotton 4 ply*:
    1 x 100g ball in lilac (shade no. 01701)
- Pair of 2mm (US 0) knitting needles
- 2 buttons

Tension and finished size
- 35 stitches and 64 rows to 10cm (4in) over garter stitch using 2mm (US 0) needles.
- Slipper measures 11cm (4½in) from toe to heel.

Slippers (make 2)
With 2mm (US 0) needles, cast on 22 sts.
Starting with a RS row, work in garter st, inc 1 st at each end of first and foll 7 alt rows (38 sts).
Work 1 row, ending with RS facing for next row.
Dec 1 st at each end of next and foll 7 alt rows, ending with **WS** facing for next row (22 sts).
This section forms the sole.
Cast on 8 sts (for heel) at beg of next row (30 sts).
Inc 1 st at beg of next and foll 7 alt rows, ending with **WS** facing for next row (38 sts).
Cast off 20 sts (for foot opening) at beg of next row (18 sts).
Work 19 rows on these 18 sts for top of foot, ending with **WS** facing for next row.
Cast on 20 sts (for other side of foot opening) at beg of next row (38 sts).
Dec 1 st at beg of next and foll 7 alt rows, ending with **WS** facing for next row.
Cast off rem 30 sts knitways (on **WS**).

Make up
Press following instructions on ball band.
Join straight row-end edges to form heel seam. Easing in fullness of upper section, sew upper section to sole.

Strap
With RS facing and 2mm (US 0) needles, starting 9 sts before heel seam, **knit up** 9 sts to heel seam, then 9 sts beyond heel seam (18 sts).
Working in garter st, cast on 14 sts at beg of next 2 rows (46 sts).
Work 1 row, ending with RS facing for next row.
LEFT SLIPPER ONLY
Next row K2, cast off 3 sts (to make buttonhole), k to end.
RIGHT SLIPPER ONLY
Next row K to last 5 sts, cast off 3 sts (to make buttonhole), k to end.
BOTH SLIPPERS
Next row K to end, casting on 3 sts over those cast off on previous row.
Work 3 rows, ending with **WS** facing for next row.
Cast off knitways (on **WS**).
Sew on buttons.

Girl's bolero

✪ *This ballet-style, wrap-over top is simply a great style to wear, doubling up for ballet practice and for parties.*

You will need
- *Patons Diploma Gold DK*:
  4 [**5**, 6, **6**, 7] x 50g balls in rose pink (shade no. 06123 or 06139)
- Pair each of 3¼mm (US 3) and 4mm (US 6) knitting needles

Tension and finished size
- 22 stitches and 30 rows to 10cm (4in) over stocking stitch using 4mm (US 6) needles.
- To fit approx age 3-4 [**4-5**, 6-7, **8-9**, 10-11] years.
- To fit chest 56 [**61**, 66, **71**, 76]cm (22 [**24**, 26, **28**, 30]in).
- Actual measurement – 59 [**65**, 70, **75**, 83]cm (23 [**25½**, 27½, **29½**, 32½]in).
- Finished length – 30 [**32**, 36, **39**, 41]cm (12 [**12½**, 14, **15½**, 16]in).
- Sleeve length – 23 [**27**, 31, **35**, 39]cm (9 [**10½**, 12, **14**, 15½]in).

Left front
With 3¼mm (US 3) needles, cast on 52 [**58**, 64, **70**, 74] sts.
Rib row 1 (RS) *K1, p1; rep from * to last 2 sts, k2.
Rib row 2 *K1, p1; rep from * to end.
These 2 rows form rib.
Cont in rib for 5 [**5**, 5, **6**, 6]cm (2 [**2**, 2, **2½**, 2½]in), ending with **WS** facing for next row.
Next row (WS) Rib 3 [**4**, 4, **5**, 1], *M1 (by picking up horizontal loop lying before next st

and knitting into back of it), rib 9 [**10**, 11, **12**, 8]; rep from * to last 4 [**4**, 5, **5**, 1] sts, M1, rib to end (58 [**64**, 70, **76**, 84] sts).
Change to 4mm (US 6) needles.
Starting with a k row, work in stocking st for 4 rows, ending with RS facing for next row.
SHAPE FRONT SLOPE
Dec 1 st at end of next row, and at same edge on foll 6 [**8**, 4, **6**, 8] rows, then on every foll alt row until 37 [**42**, 46, **49**, 56] sts rem. Work 1 row, ending with RS facing for next row.
SHAPE ARMHOLE
Cast off 2 sts at beg and dec 1 st at end of next row (34 [**39**, 43, **46**, 53] sts).
Work 1 row.
Dec 1 st at each end of next and every foll alt row until 22 [**25**, 27, **30**, 33] sts rem.
Dec 1 st at front slope edge **only** on 2nd and every foll alt row until 13 [**14**, 15, **17**, 19] sts rem.
Work 5 rows, ending with RS facing for next row.
SHAPE SHOULDER
Cast off 7 [**7**, 8, **9**, 10] sts at beg of next row.
Work 1 row.
Cast off rem 6 [**7**, 7, **8**, 9] sts.

Right front
With 3¼mm (US 3) needles, cast on 52 [**58**, 64, **70**, 74] sts.
Rib row 1 (RS) K2, *p1, k1; rep from * to end.
Rib row 2 *P1, k1; rep from * to end.
These 2 rows form rib.
Complete to match Left Front, reversing

shapings, working an extra row before start of armhole and shoulder shaping.

Back

With 3¼mm (US 3) needles, cast on 57 [**63**, 69, **75**, 79] sts.

Rib row 1 (RS), K1, *p1; k1; rep from * to end.

Rib row 2 P1, *k1, p1; rep from * to end.
These 2 rows form rib.

Cont in rib for 5 [**5**, 5, **6**, 6]cm (2 [**2**, 2, **2½**, 2½]in), ending with **WS** facing for next row.

Next row (WS) Rib 4 [**4**, 3, **3**, 1], *M1, rib 7 [**8**, 9, **10**, 7]; rep from * to last 4 [**3**, 3, **2**, 1] sts, M1, rib to end (65 [**71**, 77, **83**, 91] sts).

Change to 4mm (US 6) needles.

Starting with a k row, work in stocking st until Back matches Fronts to start of armhole shaping, ending with RS facing for next row.

SHAPE ARMHOLES

Cast off 2 sts at beg of next 2 rows (61 [**67**, 73, **79**, 87] sts).

Dec 1 st at each end of next and every foll alt row until 49 [**53**, 57, **63**, 67] sts rem.

Cont straight until Back matches Fronts to start of shoulder shaping, ending with RS facing for next row.

SHAPE SHOULDERS

Cast off 7 [**7**, 8, **9**, 10] sts at beg of next 2 rows, then 6 [**7**, 7, **8**, 9] sts at beg of foll 2 rows.

Cast off rem 23 [**25**, 27, **29**, 29] sts.

Sleeves

With 3¼mm (US 3) needles, cast on 33 [**35**, 37, **39**, 41] sts.

Work in rib as for Back for 4 [**5**, 5, **6**, 6]cm (1½ [**2**, 2, **2½**, 2½]in), ending with **WS** facing for next row.

Next row (WS) Rib 3 [**3**, 3, **2**, 3], *M1, rib 7 [**5**, 8, **6**, 6]; rep from * to last 2 [**2**, 2, **1**, 2] sts, M1, rib to end (38 [**42**, 42, **46**, 48] sts).

Change to 4mm (US 6) needles.

Starting with a k row, cont in stocking st, shaping sides by inc 1 st at each end of 11th [**9th**, 13th, **13th**, 11th] and every foll 12th [**12th**, 14th, **12th**, 12th] row until there are 46 [**52**, 52, **58**, 62] sts.

Cont straight until Sleeve meas 23 [**27**, 31, **35**, 39]cm (9 [**10½**, 12, **14**, 15½]in), ending with RS facing for next row.

SHAPE TOP

Cast off 2 sts at beg of next 2 rows (42 [**48**, 48, **54**, 58] sts).

Dec 1 st at each end of next and every foll alt row to 22 [**22**, 14, **22**, 18] sts, then on every row until 8 sts rem, ending with RS facing for next row.

Cast off rem 8 sts.

Make up

Press following instructions on ball band. Join shoulder seams. Join side seams, leaving a 3cm (1in) opening in right side seam above rib. Join sleeve seams. Insert Sleeves.

Front borders (both alike)

With 3¼mm (US 3) needles, cast on 9 sts.
Row 1 (RS) K2, (p1, k1) 3 times, k1.
Row 2 (K1, p1) 4 times, k1.
Rep last 2 rows until Border, when slightly stretched, fits up front opening edge, up front slope and across to centre back neck, sewing in place as you go along and ending with RS facing for next row.
Cast off.
Join ends of Borders at centre back neck.

Ties (make 2)

With 3¼mm (US 3) needles, cast on 9 sts.
Work as for Front Borders until Tie meas 33 [**38**, 40, **45**, 50]cm (13 [**15**, 15½, **17½**, 19½]in), ending with RS facing for next row.
Cast off.
Sew ends of Ties to edges of Front Borders just above rib.
To tie bolero, slip end of left front tie through opening in right front side seam and tie at back of bolero.

Child's gloves

✪✪✪ *These cosy gloves are knitted in 4-ply yarn, fine enough not to cause irritation to sensitive young skin.*

You will need
- *Patons Diploma Gold 4 ply*:
    1 x 50g ball in **MS** – purple (shade no. 04295)
    Small amount of **C** – green (shade no. 04125)
- Set of 4 double-pointed 2³/₄mm (US 2) knitting needles

Tension and finished size
- 32 stitches and 40 rows to 10cm (4in) over stocking stitch using 2³/₄mm (US 2) needles.
- Width around hand – 13cm (5in).
- Finished length – 21cm (8¹/₂in).

Right glove
With double-pointed 2³/₄mm (US 2) needles and C, cast on 38 sts, distributing sts evenly over 3 needles (12 sts on first 2 needles and 14 sts on 3rd needle).
Break off C and join in MS.
Round 1 (RS) *K1, p1; rep from * to end.
Rep this round 23 times more.
Round 25 (RS) Rib 4, inc in next st, rib 9, inc in next st, rib 8, inc in next st, rib 9, inc in next st, rib 4 (42 sts).
SHAPE FOR THUMB
Rounds 1 to 3 P1, k4, p1, k to end.
Round 4 P1, (inc in next st, k1) twice, p1, k to end (44 sts).
Rounds 5 to 7 P1, k6, p1, k to end.

Round 8 P1, inc in next st, k3, inc in next st, k1, p1, k to end (46 sts).
Rounds 9 to 11 P1, k8, p1, k to end.
Round 12 P1, inc in next st, k5, inc in next st, k1, p1, k to end (48 sts).
Rounds 13 to 15 P1, k10, p1, k to end.
Round 16 P1, inc in next st, k7, inc in next st, k1, p1, k to end (50 sts).
Rounds 17 to 19 P1, k12, p1, k to end.
Round 20 K1, slip next 12 sts onto a holder for thumb, cast on 2 sts, k to end (40 sts).
Rounds 21 to 28 Knit.**
SHAPE FIRST FINGER
Next round K6, slip next 29 sts onto a holder, cast on 2 sts, k rem 5 sts (13 sts).
***Distribute these 13 sts evenly over 3 needles and proceed thus:
Next round Knit.
Rep last round 23 times more.
Next round (K2tog) 6 times, k1 (7 sts).
Next round K1, (k2tog) 3 times.
Break yarn and thread through rem 4 sts.
Pull up tight and fasten off securely.
SHAPE SECOND FINGER
Next round Rejoin yarn and k first 5 sts from holder, leave next 19 sts on holder, cast on 2 sts, k rem 5 sts on holder, then **knit up** 2 sts from base of first finger (14 sts).
Distribute these 14 sts evenly over 3 needles and proceed thus:
Next round Knit.
Rep last round 27 times more.
Next round (K2tog) 7 times (7 sts).
Next round K1, (k2tog) 3 times.
Break yarn and thread through rem 4 sts.
Pull up tight and fasten off securely.***

SHAPE THIRD FINGER

Next round Rejoin yarn and k first 4 sts from holder, leave next 10 sts on holder, cast on 2 sts, k rem 5 sts on holder, then **knit up** 2 sts from base of second finger (13 sts).
****Distribute these 13 sts evenly over 3 needles and proceed thus:
Next round Knit.
Rep last round 23 times more.
Next round (K2tog) 6 times, k1 (7 sts).
Next round K1, (k2tog) 3 times.
Break yarn and thread through rem 4 sts.
Pull up tight and fasten off securely.

SHAPE FOURTH FINGER

Next round Rejoin yarn and k 10 sts on holder, then **knit up** 2 sts from base of third finger (12 sts).
Distribute these 12 sts evenly over 3 needles and proceed thus:
Next round Knit.
Rep last round 16 times more.
Next round (K2tog) 6 times (6 sts).
Next round (K2tog) 3 times.
Break yarn and thread through rem 3 sts.
Pull up tight and fasten off securely.

SHAPE THUMB

Next round Rejoin yarn and k 12 sts on thumb holder, then **knit up** 2 sts from base of hand section (14 sts).
Distribute these 14 sts evenly over 3 needles and proceed thus:
Next round Knit.
Rep last round 14 times more.
Next round (K2tog) 7 times (7 sts).
Next round K1, (k2tog) 3 times.
Break yarn and thread through rem 4 sts.
Pull up tight and fasten off securely.

Left glove

Work as for Right Glove to **.

SHAPE FIRST FINGER

Next round K9, slip next 29 sts onto a holder, cast on 2 sts, k rem 2 sts (13 sts).
Work as for Right Glove from *** to ***.

SHAPE THIRD FINGER

Next round Rejoin yarn and k first 5 sts from holder, leave next 10 sts on holder, cast on 2 sts, k rem 4 sts on holder, then **knit up** 2 sts from base of second finger (13 sts).
Complete as for Right Glove from ****.

Make up

Press following instructions on ball band.

Child's wool cardigan

✪✪ *You can make this pattern up for a boy or girl, choosing the colours that you prefer and reversing the button band for a boy.*

You will need
- Patons Diploma Gold DK:
    5 [**5**, 6, **6**, 6, **7**] x 50g balls in desired shade
- Pair each of 3¼mm (US 3) and 4mm (US 6) knitting needles
- 5 [**5**, 6, **6**, 7, **7**] buttons

Tension and finished size
- 22 stitches and 30 rows to 10cm (4in) over stocking stitch using 4mm (US 6) needles.
- To fit approx age 2-3 [**3-4**, 4-5, **6-7**, 8-9, **10-11**] years.
- To fit chest 51 [**56**, 61, **66**, 71, **76**]cm (20 [**22**, 24, **26**, 28, **30**]in).
- Actual measurement – 58 [**64**, 69, **75**, 80, **85**]cm (23 [**25**, 27, **29½**, 31½, **33½**]in).
- Finished length – 33 [**36**, 41, **46**, 50, **54**]cm (13 [**14**, 16, **18**, 19½, **21½**]in).
- Sleeve length – 21 [**24**, 28, **32**, 36, **39**]cm (8½ [**9½**, 11, **12½**, 14, **15½**]in).

Back
With 3¼mm (US 3) needles, cast on 63 [**69**, 75, **81**, 87, **93**] sts.
Rib row 1 (RS) K1, *p1, k1; rep from * to end.
Rib row 2 P1, *k1, p1; rep from * to end.
These 2 rows form rib.
Cont in rib for 2 [**2**, 4, **4**, 5, **5**]cm (1 [**1**, 1½, **1½**, 2, **2**]in), inc 1 st at centre of last row and ending with RS facing for next row

(64 [**70**, 76, **82**, 88, **94**] sts).
Change to 4mm (US 6) needles.
Starting with a k row, cont in stocking st until Back meas 19 [**21**, 24, **28**, 31, **33**]cm (7½ [**8½**, 9½, **11**, 12, **13**]in), ending with RS facing for next row.
SHAPE RAGLAN ARMHOLES
Cast off 2 sts at beg of next 2 rows (60 [**66**, 72, **78**, 84, **90**] sts).
Next row (RS) K1, sL1K, k1, psso, k to last 3 sts, k2tog, k1.
Next row Purl.
Rep last 2 rows 19 [**21**, 23, **25**, 27, **29**] times more, ending with RS facing for next row.
Cast off rem 20 [**22**, 24, **26**, 28, **30**] sts.

Pocket linings (make 2)
With 4mm (US 6) needles, cast on 15 [**15**, 19, **19**, 23, **23**] sts.
Starting with a k row, work in stocking st for 7 [**7**, 8, **8**, 9, **9**]cm (3 [**3**, 3, **3**, 3½, **3½**]in), ending with RS facing for next row.
Break yarn and leave sts on a holder.

Left front
With 3¼mm (US 3) needles, cast on 31 [**35**, 37, **41**, 43, **47**] sts.
Work in rib as for Back for 2 [**2**, 4, **4**, 5, **5**]cm (1 [**1**, 1½, **1½**, 2, **2**]in), inc 1 [**0**, 1, **0**, 1, **0**] st at centre of last row and ending with RS facing for next row (32 [**35**, 38, **41**, 44, **47**] sts).
Change to 4mm (US 6) needles.
Starting with a k row, cont in stocking st until Left Front meas 9 [**9**, 12, **12**, 14, **14**]cm (3½ [**3½**, 4½, **4½**, 5½, **5½**]in), ending with RS facing for next row.**

PLACE POCKET

Next row (RS) K8 [**9**, 9, **10**, 10, **11**], slip next 15 [**15**, 19, **19**, 23, **23**] sts onto a holder and, in their place, k across 15 [**15**, 19, **19**, 23, **23**] sts of first Pocket Lining, k to end.

Cont straight until Left Front matches Back to start of raglan armhole shaping, ending with RS facing for next row.

SHAPE RAGLAN ARMHOLE AND FRONT SLOPE

Next row (RS) Cast off 2 sts, k to last 3 sts, k2tog, k1 (29 [**32**, 35, **38**, 41, **44**] sts).

Working all front slope decreases as set by last row and all raglan armhole decreases as set by Back, dec 1 st at raglan armhole edge of 2nd and every foll alt row **and at same time** dec 1 st at front slope edge on 4th and every foll 4th row until 8 sts rem.

Dec 1 st at raglan armhole edge **only** on 2nd and every foll alt row until 2 sts rem.

Work 1 row, ending with RS facing for next row.

Next row (RS) K2tog and fasten off.

Right front

Work as for Left Front to **.

PLACE POCKET

Next row (RS) K9 [**11**, 10, **12**, 11, **13**], slip next 15 [**15**, 19, **19**, 23, **23**] sts onto a holder and, in their place, k across 15 [**15**, 19, **19**, 23, **23**] sts of second Pocket Lining, k to end.

Complete to match Left Front, reversing shapings, working an extra row before start of raglan armhole shaping.

Sleeves

With 3¼mm (US 3) needles, cast on 31 [**33**, 35, **35**, 37, **39**] sts.

Work in rib as for Back for 2 [**2**, 4, **4**, 5, **5**]cm (1 [**1**, 1½, **1½**, 2, **2**]in), inc 3 sts evenly across last row and ending with RS facing for next row (34 [**36**, 38, **38**, 40, **42**] sts).

Change to 4mm (US 6) needles.

Starting with a k row, cont in stocking st, shaping sides by inc 1 st at each end of 9th [**9th**, next, **9th**, 3rd, **3rd**] and every foll 10th [**10th**, 10th, **10th**, 11th, **11th**] row until there are 44 [**48**, 52, **52**, 56, **60**] sts.

Cont straight until Sleeve meas 21 [**24**, 28, **32**, 36, **39**]cm (8½ [**9½**, 11, **12½**, 14, **15½**]in), ending with RS facing for next row.

SHAPE RAGLAN

Cast off 2 sts at beg of next 2 rows (40 [**44**, 48, **48**, 52, **56**] sts).

Work 2 rows.

Working all raglan decreases as set by Back, dec 1 st at each end of next and every foll 4th row until 34 [**38**, 42, **38**, 42, **46**] sts rem, then on every foll alt row until 6 sts rem.

Work 1 row, ending with RS facing for next row. Cast off rem 6 sts.

Make up

Press following instructions on ball band. Join raglan seams.

Button border

With 3¼mm (US 3) needles, cast on 7 sts.

Row 1 (RS) K2, (p1, k1) twice, k1.

Row 2 (K1, p1) 3 times, k1.

Rep last 2 rows until Border, when slightly stretched, fits up front opening edge (left front for a girl, or right front for a boy), up front slope and across to centre back neck, sewing in place as you go along and ending with RS facing for next row. Cast off.

Mark positions for 5 [**5**, 6, **6**, 7, **7**] buttons on this Border – first to come 1cm (³⁄₈in) up from cast-on edge, last to come level with start of front slope shaping, and rem 3 [**3**, 4, **4**, 5, **5**] buttons evenly spaced between.

Buttonhole border

Work to match Button Border, with the addition of 5 [**5**, 6, **6**, 7, **7**] buttonholes worked to correspond with positions marked for buttons.

FOR A GIRL:

To make a buttonhole On a RS row, rib 3, cast off 2 sts, rib to end; then rib back, casting on 2 sts over those cast off on previous row.

FOR A BOY:

To make a buttonhole On a RS row, rib 2, cast off 2 sts, rib to end; then rib back, casting on 2 sts over those cast off on previous row.

FOR BOTH A GIRL AND A BOY:

Join ends of Borders at centre back neck.

Pocket tops (both alike)

Slip 15 [**15**, 19, **19**, 23, **23**] sts from pocket holder onto 3¼mm (US 3) needles and rejoin yarn with RS facing.

Starting with rib row 1, work in rib as for Back for 4 [**4**, 6, **6**, 8, **8**] rows, ending with RS facing for next row.

Cast off in rib.

Sew Pocket Linings in place on inside, then neatly sew down ends of Pocket Tops. Join side and sleeve seams. Sew on buttons.

Child's cotton sweaters

✪ *These classic sweater patterns, knitted in cotton yarn, are worked here in children's sizes – covering ages three to thirteen. They are great for all-year-round wear. Work the V-neck version or the round-neck version, or make one of each.*

You will need

- *Patons 100% Cotton 4 ply*:
  3 [**3**, 3, **3**, 4, **4**] x 100g balls in **MS** – denim blue (shade no. 01697) or blue-green (shade no. 01705)
  1 x 100g ball in **C** – light purple (shade no 01710) or brick red (shade no. 01709)
- Pair each of 2³⁄4mm (US 2) and 3¹⁄4mm (US 3) knitting needles

Tension and finished size

- 28 stitches and 36 rows to 10cm (4in) over stocking stitch using 3¹⁄4mm (US 3) needles.
- To fit approx age 3-4 [**4-5**, 6-7, **8-9**, 10-11, **12-13**] years.
- To fit chest 56 [**61**, 66, **71**, 76, **81**]cm (22 [**24**, 26, **28**, 30, **32**]in).
- Actual measurement – 64 [**69**, 74, **79**, 84, **89**]cm (25 [**27**, 29, **31**, 33, **35**]in).
- Finished length – 37 [**41**, 45, **48**, 51, **54**]cm (14¹⁄2 [**16**, 17¹⁄2, **19**, 20, **21¹⁄2**]in).
- Sleeve length – 25 [**29**, 33, **37**, 39, **42**]cm (10 [**11¹⁄2**, 13, **14¹⁄2**, 15¹⁄2, **16¹⁄2**]in).

V-NECK SWEATER

Back

With 2³⁄4mm (US 2) needles and C, cast on 83 [**89**, 97, **103**, 111, **117**] sts.

Break off C and join in MS.

Rib row 1 (RS) K1, *p1, k1; rep from * to end.
Rib row 2 P1, *k1, p1; rep from * to end.
These 2 rows form rib.
Cont in rib for 5 [**5**, 5, **5**, 6, **6**]cm (2 [**2**, 2, **2**, 2¹⁄2, **2¹⁄2**]in), ending with **WS** facing for next row.
Next row (WS) Rib 5 [**5**, 6, 6, 7, 7], * M1 (by picking up horizontal loop lying before next st and knitting into back of it), rib 12 [**13**, 14, **15**, 16, **17**]; rep from * to last 6 [**6**, 7, **7**, 8, **8**] sts, M1, rib to end (90 [**96**, 104, **110**, 118, **124**] sts).
Change to 3¹⁄4mm (US 3) needles.
Starting with a k row, cont in stocking st until Back meas 21 [**24**, 27, **29**, 30, **32**]cm (8¹⁄2 [**9¹⁄2**, 10¹⁄2, **11¹⁄2**, 12, **12¹⁄2**]in), ending with RS facing for next row.
SHAPE RAGLAN ARMHOLES
Cast off 2 sts at beg of next 2 rows (86 [**92**, 100, **106**, 114, **120**] sts).
Next row (RS) K1, sL1K, k1, psso, k to last 3 sts, k2tog, k1 (84 [**90**, 98, **104**, 112, **118**] sts).
Next row Purl.**
Rep last 2 rows 23 [**25**, 28, **30**, 33, **35**] times more, ending with RS facing for next row (38 [**40**, 42, **44**, 46, **48**] sts).
Next row (RS) K1, sL1K, k2tog, psso, k to last 4 sts, k3tog, k1.
Next row Purl.
Rep last 2 rows twice more.
Break yarn and leave rem 26 [**28**, 30, **32**, 34, **36**] sts on a holder.

Front

Work as for Back to **.

DIVIDE FOR NECK

Next row (RS) K1, sL1K, k1, psso, k36 [**39**, 43, **46**, 50, **53**], k2tog, k1, turn and work this side first.

Working all raglan decreases as set by Back and all neck decreases as set by last row, proceed thus:

Dec 1 st at raglan armhole edge on 2nd and foll 21 [**23**, 26, **28**, 30, **32**] alt rows and **at same time** dec 1 st at neck edge on 4th and every foll 4th row (7 [**7**, 7, **7**, 8, **8**] sts).

76 and 81cm (30 and 32in) sizes only: Dec 1 st at raglan armhole edge **only** on 2nd row (7 sts).

All sizes: Working raglan armhole decreases as set by Back, dec 2 sts at raglan armhole edge **only** on 2nd and foll alt row (3 sts).

Work 1 row, ending with RS facing for next row.

Next row (RS) SL1K, k2tog, psso.

Next row P1 and fasten off.

With RS facing, rejoin yarn to rem sts, k1, sL1K, k1, psso, k to last 3 sts, k2tog, k1 (40 [**43**, 47, **50**, 54, **57**] sts).

Complete to match first side, reversing shapings.

Sleeves

With 2³⁄4mm (US 2) needles and C, cast on 45 [**47**, 49, **51**, 53, **55**] sts.

Break off C and join in MS.

Work in rib as for Back for 5 [**5**, 5, **5**, 6, **6**]cm (2 [**2**, 2, **2**, 2¹⁄2, **2¹⁄2**]in), ending with **WS** facing for next row.

Next row (WS) Rib 7 [**7**, 8, **5**, 4, **5**], * M1, rib 15 [**16**, 16, **10**, 11, **11**]; rep from * to last 8 [**8**, 9, **6**, 5, **6**] sts, M1, rib to end (48 [**50**, 52, **56**, 58, **60**] sts).

Change to 3¹⁄4mm (US 3) needles.

Starting with a k row, cont in stocking st, shaping sides by inc 1 st at each end of 3rd [**3rd**, 3rd, **7th**, 3rd, **3rd**] and every foll 7th row

to 62 [**60**, 68, **68**, 70, **70**] sts, then on every foll 8th row until there are 66 [**70**, 76, **80**, 86, **90**] sts.

Cont straight until Sleeve meas 25 [**29**, 33, **37**, 39, **42**]cm (10 [**11¹⁄2**, 13, **14¹⁄2**, 15¹⁄2, **16¹⁄2**]in), ending with RS facing for next row.

SHAPE RAGLAN

Cast off 2 sts at beg of next 2 rows (62 [**66**, 72, **76**, 82, **86**] sts).

Working all raglan decreases as set by Back, dec 1 st at each end of next and every foll alt row until 8 sts rem.

Work 1 row, ending with RS facing for next row.

Break yarn and leave rem 8 sts on a holder.

Make up

Press following instructions on ball band.
Join both front and right back raglan seams.

Neck border

With RS facing, 2³⁄4mm (US 2) needles and MS, k 8 sts from left sleeve, **knit up** 44 [**48**, 52, **54**, 60, **62**] sts down left side of neck, 1 st from base of V and mark this st with a coloured thread, and 44 [**48**, 52, **54**, 60, **62**] sts up right side of neck, k 8 sts from right sleeve, then 26 [**28**, 30, **32**, 34, **36**] sts from back (131 [**141**, 151, **157**, 171, **177**] sts).

Row 1 (WS) (P1, k1) to within 2 sts of marked st, p2tog, p marked st, p2tog tbl, (k1, p1) to end.

Row 2 K1, (p1, k1) to within 2 sts of marked st, p2tog, k marked st, p2tog tbl, k1, (p1, k1) to end.

Rep last 2 rows 3 times more, then row 1 again, ending with RS facing for next row.

Break off MS and join in C.

Using a 3¹⁄4mm (US 3) needle and C, cast off rem 113 [**123**, 133, **139**, 153, **159**] sts in rib, still decreasing either side of marked st as before.

Join left back raglan and Neck Border seam. Join side and sleeve seams.

ROUND-NECK SWEATER

Back
Work as for Back of V-Neck Sweater (starts on page 50).

Front
Work as for Back until 46 [**48**, 52, **54**, 58, **60**] sts rem in raglan armhole shaping.
Work 1 row, ending with RS facing for next row.

SHAPE NECK
Next row (RS) K1, sL1K, k1, psso, k14 [**14**, 17, **17**, 20, **20**], turn and work this side first.
Working all raglan decreases as set by Back, proceed thus:
Dec 1 st at neck edge on next 6 [**6**, 8, **8**, 10, **10**] rows **and at same time** dec 1 st at raglan armhole edge on 2nd and every foll alt row (7 sts).
Dec 2 sts at raglan armhole edge **only** on 2nd and foll alt row (3 sts).
Work 1 row, ending with RS facing for next row.
Next row (RS) SL1K, k2tog, psso.
Next row P1 and fasten off.
With RS facing, slip centre 12 [**14**, 12, **14**, 12, **14**] sts onto a holder, rejoin yarn to rem sts, k to last 3 sts, k2tog, k1 (16 [**16**, 19, **19**, 22, **22**] sts).
Complete to match first side, reversing shapings.

Sleeves
Work as for Sleeves of V-Neck Sweater.

Make up
Press following instructions on ball band.
Join both front and right back raglan seams.

Neck border
With RS facing, 2³/₄mm (US 2) needles and MS, k 8 sts from left sleeve, **knit up** 12 [**12**, 14, **14**, 16, **16**] sts down left side of neck, k 12 [**14**, 12, **14**, 12, **14**] sts from front, **knit up** 12 [**12**, 14, **14**, 16, **16**] sts up right side of neck, k 8 sts from right sleeve, then 26 [**28**, 30, **32**, 34, **36**] sts from back inc 1 st at centre (79 [**83**, 87, **91**, 95, **99**] sts).
Starting with rib row 2, work in rib as for Back for 4 [**4**, 5, **5**, 6, **6**]cm (1¹/₂ [**1¹/₂**, 2, **2**, 2¹/₂, **2¹/₂**]in), ending with RS facing for next row.
Using a 3¹/₄mm (US 3) needle, cast off in rib.
Join left back raglan and Neck Border seam.
Fold Neck Border in half to inside and stitch in place. Join side and sleeve seams.

Child's raglan sweaters

✪ *Knitted in machine-washable, double-knitting weight wool, this classic sweater has raglan sleeves and a simple k1, p1 rib at the neck, hem and cuffs. It is one of the simplest garments to knit. To create a perfect neckline, read how to pick up stitches evenly on page 23.*

You will need

- *Patons Diploma Gold DK*:
  For Round-Neck Sweater, 5 [**5**, 6, **6**, 7] x 50g balls in rose pink (shade no. 06123) or light lime (shade no. 06236) – you will need one extra ball for Polo-Neck Sweater
- Pair each of 3¹⁄₄mm (US 3) and 4mm (US 6) knitting needles

Tension and finished size

- 22 stitches and 30 rows to 10cm (4in) over stocking stitch using 4mm (US 6) needles.
- To fit approx age 3-4 [**4-5**, 6-7, **8-9**, 10-11] years.
- To fit chest 56 [**61**, 66, **71**, 76]cm (22 [**24**, 26, **28**, 30]in).
- Actual measurement – 60 [**65**, 71, **76**, 82]cm (23¹⁄₂ [**25¹⁄₂**, 28, **30**, 32¹⁄₂]in).
- Finished length – 42 [**44**, 46, **49**, 52]cm (16¹⁄₂ [**17¹⁄₂**, 18, **19¹⁄₂**, 20¹⁄₂]in).
- Sleeve length – 27 [**30**, 34, **38**, 42]cm (10¹⁄₂ [**12**, 13¹⁄₂, **15**, 16¹⁄₂]in).

Back

With 3¹⁄₄mm (US 3) needles, cast on 65 [**71**, 77, **83**, 89] sts.
Rib row 1 (RS) K1, *p1, k1; rep from * to end.
Rib row 2 P1, *k1, p1; rep from * to end.

These 2 rows form rib.
Cont in rib for 5 [**5**, 5, **6**, 6]cm (2 [**2**, 2, **2¹⁄₂**, 2¹⁄₂]in), inc 1 st at centre of last row and ending with RS facing for next row (66 [**72**, 78, **84**, 90] sts).
Change to 4mm (US 6) needles.
Starting with a k row, cont in stocking st until Back meas 27 [**28**, 29, **30**, 32]cm (10¹⁄₂ [**11**, 11¹⁄₂, **12**, 12¹⁄₂]in), ending with RS facing for next row.
SHAPE RAGLAN ARMHOLES
Cast off 1 [**2**, 2, **3**, 4] sts at beg of next 2 rows (64 [**68**, 74, **78**, 82] sts).
Next row (RS) K1, sL1K, k1, psso, k to last 3 sts, k2tog, k1.
Next row K1, p to last st, k1.
Rep last 2 rows 17 [**19**, 21, **23**, 25] times more, ending with RS facing for next row (28 [**28**, 30, **30**, 30] sts).
SHAPE BACK NECK
Next row (RS) K1, sL1K, k1, psso, k4, turn and work this side first.
Dec 1 st at neck edge on next 3 rows **and at same time** dec 1 st at raglan armhole edge on 2nd row (2 sts).
Next row (RS) K2tog.
Next row P1 and fasten off.
With RS facing, slip centre 14 [**14**, 16, **16**, 16] sts onto a holder, rejoin yarn to rem sts, k to last 3 sts, k2tog, k1 (6 sts).
Complete to match first side, reversing shapings.

Front

Work as for Back until 32 [**34**, 34, **36**, 38] sts rem in raglan armhole shaping.

Work 1 row, ending with RS facing for next row.

SHAPE FRONT NECK

Next row (RS) K1, sL1K, k1, psso, k8 [**9**, 8, **9**, 10], turn and work this side first.

Dec 1 st at neck edge on next 5 rows **and at same time** dec 1 st at raglan armhole edge on 2nd and foll alt row [3 [**4**, 3, **4**, 5] sts].

Dec 1 st at raglan armhole edge **only** on next and foll 0 [**1**, 0, **1**, 2] alt rows (2 sts).

Work 1 row, ending with RS facing for next row.

Next row (RS) K2tog.

Next row P1 and fasten off.

With RS facing, slip centre 10 [**10**, 12, **12**, 12] sts onto a holder, rejoin yarn to rem sts, k to last 3 sts, k2tog, k1 (10 [**11**, 10, **11**, 12] sts). Complete to match first side, reversing shapings.

Sleeves

With 3¼mm (US 3) needles, cast on 33 [**33**, 35, **37**, 39] sts.

Work in rib as for Back for 6cm (2½in), ending with **WS** facing for next row.

Next row (WS) Rib 2 [**2**, 3, **2**, 3], *M1, rib 7 [**7**, 7, **8**, 8]; rep from * to last 3 [**3**, 4, **3**, 4] sts, M1, rib to end (38 [**38**, 40, **42**, 44] sts).

Change to 4mm (US 6) needles.

Starting with a k row, cont in stocking st, shaping sides by inc 1 st at each end of 5th [**5th**, 7th, **5th**, 3rd] and every foll 8th [**7th**, 7th, **7th**, 7th] row until there are 50 [**56**, 60, **66**, 72] sts.

Cont straight until Sleeve meas 27 [**30**, 34, **38**, 42]cm (10½ [**12**, 13½, **15**, 16½]in), ending with RS facing for next row.

SHAPE RAGLAN

Cast off 1 [**2**, 2, **3**, 4] sts at beg of next 2 rows (48 [**52**, 56, **60**, 64] sts).

Working all raglan decreases as set by Back, dec 1 st at each end of next and

every foll alt row until 6 sts rem.

Work 1 row, ending with RS facing for next row.

Break yarn and leave rem 6 sts on a holder.

Make up

Press following instructions on ball band.

Join both front and right back raglan seams.

Neck border

With RS facing and 3¼mm (US 3) needles, k 6 sts from left sleeve, **knit up** 10 [**11**, 11, **13**, 14] sts down left side of front neck, k 10 [**10**, 12, **12**, 12] sts from front inc 3 sts evenly, **knit up** 10 [**11**, 11, **13**, 14] sts up right side of front neck, k 6 sts from right sleeve, **knit up** 5 [**6**, 6, **6**, 6] sts down right side of back neck, k 14 [**14**, 16, **16**, 16] sts from back inc 4 sts evenly, then **knit up** 5 [**6**, 6, **6**, 6] sts up left side of back neck (73 [**77**, 81, **85**, 87] sts).

ROUND-NECK SWEATER ONLY:

Starting with rib row 2, work in rib as for Back for 4 [**5**, 5, **6**, 7]cm (1½ [**2**, 2, **2½**, 3]in). Using a 4mm (US 6) needle, cast off in rib. Join left back raglan and Neck Border seam. Fold Neck Border in half to inside and stitch in place. Join side and sleeve seams.

POLO-NECK SWEATER ONLY:

Starting with rib row 1, work in rib as for Back for 10 [**12**, 12, **12**, 14]cm (4 [**4½**, 4½, **4½**, 5½]in).

Using a 4mm (US 6) needle, cast off in rib. Join left back raglan and Neck Border seam, reversing Neck Border seam for last 5 [**6**, 6, **6**, 7]cm (2 [**2½**, 2½, **2½**, 3]in) for turn-back. Join side and sleeve seams.

Unisex V-neck sweater

⭐ *This cool cotton sweater looks good on both sexes. Tipping the V-neck, cuffs and ribs in a contrasting colour gives it a touch of class.*

You will need
- *Patons 100% Cotton 4 ply*:
  5 [**5**, 5, **5**, 6, **6**] x 100g balls in **MS** – brick red (shade no. 01709)
  1 x 100g ball in **C** – red (shade no. 01708)
- Pair each of 2³/₄mm (US 2) and 3¹/₄mm (US 3) knitting needles

Tension and finished size
- 28 stitches and 36 rows to 10cm (4in) over stocking stitch using 3¹/₄mm (US 3) needles.
- To fit bust/chest 81 [**86**, 91, **97**, 102, **107**]cm (32 [**34**, 36, **38**, 40, **42**]in).
- Actual measurement – 88 [**92**, 98, **102**, 108, **112**]cm (34¹/₂ [**36**, 38¹/₂, **40**, 42¹/₂, **44**]in).
- Finished length – 64 [**65**, 67, **68**, 69, **70**]cm (25 [**25¹/₂**, 26¹/₂, **27**, 27, **27¹/₂**]in).
- Sleeve length – 43 [**43**, 44, **44**, 46, **46**]cm (17 [**17**, 17¹/₂, **17¹/₂**, 18, **18**]in).

Back
With 2³/₄mm (US 2) needles and C, cast on 117 [**123**, 131, **137**, 145, **151**] sts.
Break off C and join in MS.
Rib row 1 (RS) K1, *p1, k1; rep from * to end.
Rib row 2 P1, *k1, p1; rep from * to end.
These 2 rows form rib.
Cont in rib for 5cm (2in), ending with **WS** facing for next row.
Next row (WS) Rib 8 [**9**, 10, **11**, 12, **13**], *M1 (by picking up horizontal loop lying before

next st and knitting into back of it), rib 20 [**21**, 22, **23**, 24, **25**]; rep from * to last 9 [**9**, 11, **11**, 13, **13**] sts, M1, rib to end (123 [**129**, 137, **143**, 151, **157**] sts).
Change to 3¹/₄mm (US 3) needles.
Starting with a k row, cont in stocking st until Back meas 42cm (16¹/₂in), ending with RS facing for next row.

SHAPE RAGLAN ARMHOLES
Cast off 2 sts at beg of next 2 rows (119 [**125**, 133, **139**, 147, **153**] sts).
Next row (RS) K1, k2tog, k to last 3 sts, sL1K, k1, psso, k1.
Working all raglan armhole decreases as set by last row, dec 1 st at each end of 4th [**4th**, 4th, **2nd**, 2nd, **2nd**] and every foll alt row until 43 [**45**, 47, **47**, 53, **55**] sts rem.
Work 1 row, ending with RS facing for next row.
102 and 107cm (40 and 42in) sizes only:
Next row (RS) K1, k2tog, k to last 3 sts, sL1K, k1, psso, k1.
Next row P1, p2tog tbl, p to last 3 sts, p2tog, p1 ([49, **51**] sts).
All sizes:
Break yarn and leave rem 43 [**45**, 47, **47**, 49, **51**] sts on a holder.

Front
Work as for Back until 109 [**115**, 123, **127**, 135, **141**] sts rem in raglan armhole shaping.
Work 1 row, ending with RS facing for next row.

DIVIDE FOR NECK
Next row (RS) K1, k2tog, k51 [**54**, 58, **60**, 64, **67**], turn and work this side first.

Working all raglan armhole decreases as set, dec 1 st at raglan armhole edge on 2nd and every foll alt row **and at same time** dec 1 st at neck edge on next and every foll 3rd row until 7 [**7**, 9, **11**, 12, **13**] sts rem.

Dec 1 st at raglan armhole edge **only** on next [**2nd**, next, **next**, 2nd, **next**] and every foll alt row until 2 [**2**, 2, **2**, 3, **3**] sts rem, ending with **WS** facing for next row.

81, 86, 91 and 97cm (32, 34, 36 and 38in) sizes only:
Work 1 row.

102 and 107cm (40 and 42in) sizes only:
Next row (WS) P2tog, p1.

All sizes:
Next row K2tog and fasten off.
With RS facing, slip centre st onto a holder, rejoin yarn to rem sts, k to last 3 sts, sL1K, k1, psso, k1 (53 [**56**, 60, **62**, 66, **69**] sts).
Complete to match first side, reversing shapings.

Sleeves

With 2³/₄mm (US 2) needles and C, cast on 57 [**59**, 61, **61**, 63, **65**] sts.
Break off C and join in MS.
Work in rib as for Back for 5cm (2in), inc 1 st at centre of last row and ending with RS facing for next row (58 [**60**, 62, **62**, 64, **66**] sts).
Change to 3¹/₄mm (US 3) needles.
Starting with a k row, cont in stocking st, shaping sides by inc 1 st at each end of 7th [**3rd**, 9th, **5th**, 3rd, **9th**] and every foll 8th [**8th**, 7th, **7th**, 7th, **6th**] row until there are 88 [**92**, 96, **98**, 102, **106**] sts.
Cont straight until Sleeve meas 43 [**43**, 44, **44**, 46, **46**]cm (17 [**17**, 17¹/₂, **17¹/₂**, 18, **18**]in), ending with RS facing for next row.
SHAPE RAGLAN
Cast off 2 sts at beg of next 2 rows (84 [**88**, 92, **94**, 98, **102**] sts).
Working all raglan armhole decreases as set

by Back, dec 1 st at each end of next and 0 [**0**, 1, **2**, 2, **2**] foll 4th rows, then on every foll alt row until 6 sts rem.
Work 1 row, ending with RS facing for next row.
Break yarn and leave rem 6 sts on a holder.

Make up
Press following instructions on ball band.
Join both front and right back raglan seams.

Neck border
With RS facing, 2³/₄mm (US 2) needles and MS, k 6 sts from left sleeve, **knit up** 60 [**66**, 70, **74**, 80, **84**] sts down left side of neck, k st left on holder at base of V and mark this st with a coloured thread, **knit up** 60 [**66**, 70, **74**, 80, **84**] sts up right side of neck, k 6 sts from right sleeve, then k 43 [**45**, 47, **47**, 49, **51**] sts from back inc 3 sts evenly (179 [**193**, 203, **211**, 225, **235**] sts).
Row 1 (WS) (P1, k1) to within 2 sts of marked st, p2tog, p marked st, p2tog tbl, (k1, p1) to end.
Row 2 K1, (p1, k1) to within 2 sts of marked st, p2tog, k marked st, p2tog tbl, k1, (p1, k1) to end.
Rep last 2 rows 3 times more, then row 1 again, ending with RS facing for next row.
Break off MS and join in C.
Using a 3¹/₄mm (US 3) needle, cast off rem 161 [**175**, 185, **193**, 207, **217**] sts in rib, still decreasing either side of marked st as before.
Join left back raglan and Neck Border seam.
Join side and sleeve seams.

Bobble hats

✪✪ *In four sizes, you can make these for all the family. Pick toning colours for the ribbing and the main body of the hat. Make the pompoms small or large, in desired colours.*

You will need

- *Patons Diploma Gold DK*:
  1 [**1**: 2: **2**] x 50g balls each in **MS** for hat and in **C** for ribbing
  1 x 50g ball in extra colour for contrasting pompom (optional)
- Pair each of 3¼mm (US 3) and 4mm (US 6) knitting needles

Tension and finished size

- 22 stitches and 30 rows to 10cm (4in) over stocking stitch using 4mm (US 6) needles.
- To fit 7-10 years [**11-14 years**, lady, **man**].
- Width around head – 46 [**50**, 55, **58**]cm (18 [**19¹⁄₂**, 21¹⁄₂, **23**]in).

To make

With 3¼mm (US 3) needles and C, cast on 101 [**111**, 121, **127**] sts.
Rib row 1 (RS) K1, *p1, k1; rep from * to end.
Rib row 2 P1, *k1, p1; rep from * to end.
These 2 rows form rib.
Cont in rib for 10 [**13**, 15, **18**]cm (4 [**5**, 6, **7**]in), ending with RS facing for next row.
Break off C and join in MS.
Change to 4mm (US 6) needles.
Starting with a k row, work in stocking st until Hat meas 15 [**18**, 20, **23**]cm (6 [**7**, 8, **9**]in), ending with RS facing for next row.
SHAPE CROWN
Row 1 (RS) K8 [**9**, 10, **13**], k2tog, (k8 [**9**, 10, **10**], k2tog) 8 times, k8 [**9**, 10, **13**], k2tog, k1 (91 [101, 111, 117] sts).
Row 2 and every foll alt row Purl.
Row 3 K7 [**8**, 9, **12**], k2tog, (k7 [**8**, 9, **9**], k2tog) 8 times, k7 [**8**, 9, **12**], k2tog, k1 (81 [**91**, 101, **107**] sts).
Row 5 K6 [**7**, 8, **11**], k2tog, (k6 [**7**, 8, **8**], k2tog) 8 times, k6 [**7**, 8, **11**], k2tog, k1 (71 [**81**, 91, **97**] sts).
Row 7 K5 [**6**, 7, **10**], k2tog, (k5 [**6**, 7, **7**], k2tog) 8 times, k5 [**6**, 7, **10**], k2tog, k1 (61 [**71**, 81, **87**] sts).
Row 9 K4 [**5**, 6, **9**], k2tog, (k4 [**5**, 6, **6**], k2tog)

8 times, k4 [**5**, 6, **9**], k2tog, k1 (51 [**61**, 71, **77**] sts).
Row 11 K3 [**4**, 5, **8**], k2tog, (k3 [**4**, 5, **5**], k2tog) 8 times, k3 [**4**, 5, **8**], k2tog, k1 (41 [**51**, 61, **67**] sts).
Row 13 K2 [**3**, 4, **7**], k2tog, (k2 [**3**, 4, **4**], k2tog) 8 times, k2 [**3**, 4, **7**], k2tog, k1 (31 [**41**, 51, **57**] sts).
Row 15 K1 [**2**, 3, **6**], k2tog, (k1 [**2**, 3, **3**], k2tog) 8 times, k1 [**2**, 3, **6**], k2tog, k1 (21 [**31**, 41, **47**] sts).
11-14 years, lady's and men's sizes only:
Row 17 K[1, 2, **5**], k2tog, (k[**1**, 2, **2**], k2tog) 8 times, k[1, 2, **5**], k2tog, k1 ([**21**, 31, **37**] sts).
Lady's and men's sizes only:
Row 19 K[1, **4**], k2tog, (k1, k2tog) 8 times, k[1, **4**], k2tog, k1 ([21, **27**] sts).

All sizes:
Next row (WS) Purl.
Next row (K3tog) 0 [**0**, 0, **3**] times, (k2tog) 10 [**10**, 10, **4**] times, (k3tog) 0 [**0**, 0, **3**] times, k1. Break yarn and thread through rem 11 sts. Pull up tight and fasten off securely.

Make up

Press following instructions on ball band. Join back seam, reversing seam for first 5 [**6**, 7, **8**]cm (2 [**2½**, 3, **3**]in) for turn-back. Make a pompom in desired colours. Wind yarn around a piece of cardboard (width of desired pompom) until it is well covered. Slip yarn off cardboard and tie at centre. Cut ends and fluff out pompom. Attach to crown of hat.

Cable sports sweater

✪✪✪ *This cable design with contrast trim at the neck and at the sleeves looks good on both men and women. Make it in traditional white, or choose more funky colours!*

You will need
- *Patons Diploma Gold DK*:
    11 [**12**, 12] x 50g balls in **MS** – off-white (shade no. 06142)
    1 x 50g ball in **C** – denim (shade no. 06136)
- Pair each of 3¼mm (US 3) and 4mm (US 6) knitting needles
- Cable needle

Tension and finished size
- 22 stitches and 30 rows to 10cm (4in) over stocking stitch using 4mm (US 6) needles.
- Cable panel (26 stitches) measures 8.5cm (3¼in).
- To fit bust/chest 76-81 [**86-91**, 97-102]cm (30-32 [**34-36**, 38-40]in).
- Actual measurement – 87 [**98**, 109]cm (34½ [**38½**, 43]in).
- Finished length – 61 [**63**, 66]cm (24 [**25**, 26]in).
- Sleeve length – 43 [**45**, 46]cm (17 [**17½**, 18]in).

Special abbreviations
C8F = slip next 4 sts onto cable needle and leave at front of work, k4, then k4 from cable needle.

C8B = slip next 4 sts onto cable needle and leave at back of work, k4, then k4 from cable needle.

Back
With 3¼mm (US 3) needles and MS, cast on 103 [**115**, 127] sts.
Beg rib on next row thus:
**Rib row 1 (RS) K1, *p1, k1; rep from * to end.
Rib row 2 P1, *k1, p1; rep from * to end.
These 2 rows form rib.
Work in rib for a further 6 rows, ending with RS facing for next row.
Join in C.
Row 9 (RS) Using C, knit.
Using C and starting with rib row 2, work in rib for 3 rows, ending with RS facing for next row.
Break off C and cont using MS **only**.
Row 13 (RS) Knit.**
Starting with rib row 2, cont in rib for a further 7 rows, ending with RS facing for next row.
Change to 4mm (US 6) needles and **patt** thus:
Row 1 (RS) K3, (p1, k5) 6 [**7**, 8] times, (p3, k8) twice, p3, (k5, p1) 6 [**7**, 8] times, k3.
Row 2 and every foll alt row P39 [**45**, 51], (k3, p8) twice, k3, p to end.
Rows 3, 5, 7 and 9 As row 1.
Row 11 K3, (p1, k5) 6 [**7**, 8] times, p3, C8F, p3, C8B, p3, (k5, p1) 6 [**7**, 8] times, k3.
Row 12 As row 2.
These 12 rows form patt.
Cont in patt until Back meas 42cm (16½in), ending with RS facing for next row.
SHAPE RAGLAN ARMHOLES
Keeping patt correct, cast off 9 sts at beg of next 2 rows (85 [**97**, 109] sts).

Next row (RS) K2, sL1K, k2tog, psso, patt to last 5 sts, k3tog, k2 (81 [**93**, 105] sts).
Next row P3, patt to last 3 sts, p3.
Next row K3, patt to last 3 sts, k3.
Next row P3, patt to last 3 sts, p3.
Rep last 4 rows 12 [**14**, 16] times more, then first 2 of these rows again, ending with RS facing for next row.
Cast off rem 29 [**33**, 37] sts.

Front

Work as for Back until 8 rows less have been worked than on Back to start of raglan armhole shaping, ending with RS facing for next row.

DIVIDE FOR NECK

Next row (RS) Patt 51 [**57**, 63] sts, turn and work this side first.
Keeping patt correct, dec 1 st at neck edge on 2nd and foll 4th row (49 [**55**, 61] sts).
Work 1 row, ending with RS facing for next row.

SHAPE RAGLAN ARMHOLE

Keeping patt correct, cast off 9 sts at beg of next row (40 [**46**, 52] sts).
Work 1 row.
Working all raglan decreases as set by Back, dec 2 sts at raglan armhole edge of next and every foll 4th row **and at same time** dec 1 st at neck edge on next and every foll 4th row until 7 sts rem.
Dec 2 sts at raglan armhole edge **only** on 4th and foll 4th row (3 sts).
Work 3 rows, ending with RS facing for next row.
Next row (RS) K3tog.
Next row P1 and fasten off.
With RS facing, slip centre st onto a holder, rejoin yarn to rem sts, patt to end (51 [**57**, 63] sts).
Complete to match first side, reversing shapings.

Sleeves

With 3¼mm (US 3) needles and MS, cast on 45 [**49**, 53] sts.
Work as for Back from ** to **.
Starting with rib row 2, cont in rib for a further 6 rows, ending with **WS** facing for next row.
Row 20 (WS) Rib 4 [**2**, 6], *inc in next st, rib 3 [**3**, 2]; rep from * to last 5 [**3**, 8] sts, inc in next st, rib to end (55 [**61**, 67] sts).
Change to 4mm (US 6) needles and **patt** thus:
Row 1 (RS) K3 [**0**, 3], (p1, k5) 2 [**3**, 3] times, (p3, k8) twice, p3, (k5, p1) 2 [**3**, 3] times, k3 [**0**, 3].
Row 2 P15 [**18**, 21], (k3, p8) twice, k3, p to end.
Rows 3 to 10 As rows 1 and 2, 4 times.
Row 11 Inc in first st, k2 [**5**, 2], (p1, k5) 2 [**2**, 3] times, p3, C8F, p3, C8B, p3, (k5, p1) 2 [**2**, 3] times, k2 [**5**, 2], inc in last st (57 [**63**, 69] sts).
Row 12 P16 [**19**, 22], (k3, p8) twice, k3, p to end.
These 12 rows form patt and start sleeve shaping.
Cont in patt, shaping sides by inc 1 st at each end of 5th and every foll 6th row to 79 [**87**, 95] sts, then on every foll 5th row until there are 87 [**95**, 103] sts, taking inc sts into patt.
Cont straight until Sleeve meas 43 [**45**, 46]cm (17 [**17½**, 18]in), ending with RS facing for next row.

SHAPE TOP

Keeping patt correct, cast off 9 sts at beg of next 2 rows (69 [**77**, 85] sts).
Working all raglan decreases as set by Back, dec 2 sts at each end of next and every foll 4th row until 13 sts rem.
Work 1 row, ending with RS facing for next row.
Cast off rem 13 sts.

Make up

Press following instructions on ball band. Join both front and right back raglan seams.

Neck border

With RS facing, 3¼mm (US 3) needles and MS, **knit up** 13 sts from left sleeve, 64 [**70**, 76] sts down left side of neck, k st left on holder at base of V and mark this st with a coloured thread, **knit up** 64 [**70**, 76] sts up right side of neck, 13 sts from right sleeve, then 28 [**32**, 36] sts from back (183 [**199**, 215] sts).

Row 1 (WS) K1, (p1, k1) to within 2 sts of marked st, p2tog, p marked st, p2tog tbl, k1, (p1, k1) to end.

Row 2 (P1, k1) to within 2 sts of marked st, p2tog, k marked st, p2tog tbl, (k1, p1) to end.

Row 3 As row 1 (177 [**193**, 209] sts). Join in C.

Row 4 (RS) Using C, k to within 2 sts of marked st, sL1K, k1, psso, k marked st, k2tog, k to end.

Rows 5 and 6 As rows 1 and 2 but using C.

Row 7 As row 1 but using C (169 [**185**, 201] sts).

Break off C and cont using MS only.

Row 8 As row 4 but using MS.

Rows 9 and 10 As rows 1 and 2.

Row 11 As row 1.

Using a 4mm (US 6) needle, cast off rem 161 [**177**, 193] sts in rib, still decreasing either side of marked st as before.

Join left back raglan and Neck Border seam. Join side and sleeve seams.

Woman's cotton cardigan

✪✪ *This classic slim-fitting cardigan in cotton yarn has a contrasting trim at the neck, cuffs and pocket tops. Buy buttons to match the chosen contrasting trim for a great effect.*

You will need
- *Patons 100% Cotton 4 ply*:
    4 [**5**, 5, **5**, 6, **6**] x 100g balls in **MS** – purple (shade no. 01710)
    1 x 100g ball in **C** – pink (shade no. 01706)
- Pair each of 2³/₄mm (US 2) and 3¹/₄mm (US 3) knitting needles
- 9 buttons

Tension and finished size
- 28 stitches and 36 rows to 10cm (4in) over stocking stitch using 3¹/₄mm (US 3) needles.
- To fit bust 76 [**81**, 86, **91**, 97, **102**]cm (30 [**32**, 34, **36**, 38, **40**]in).
- Actual measurement – 83 [**87**, 91, **97**, 103, **107**]cm (32¹/₂ [**34¹/₂**, 36, **38**, 40¹/₂, **42**]in).
- Finished length – 60 [**61**, 62, **63**, 65, **66**]cm (23¹/₂ [**24**, 24¹/₂, **25**, 25¹/₂, **26**]in).
- Sleeve length – 42 [**42**, 43, **43**, 43, **43**]cm (16¹/₂ [**16¹/₂**, 17, **17**, 17, **17**]in).

Back
With 2³/₄mm (US 2) needles and C, cast on 115 [**121**, 127, **135**, 143, **149**] sts.
Break off C and join in MS.
Rib row 1 (RS) K1, *p1, k1; rep from * to end.
Rib row 2 P1, *k1, p1; rep from * to end.
These 2 rows form rib.
Cont in rib for 5cm (2in), inc 1 st at centre of

last row and ending with RS facing for next row (116 [**122**, 128, **136**, 144, **150**] sts).
Change to 3¹/₄mm (US 3) needles.
Starting with a k row, cont in stocking st until Back meas 42cm (16¹/₂in), ending with RS facing for next row.
SHAPE ARMHOLES
Cast off 3 sts at beg of next 2 rows (110 [**116**, 122, **130**, 138, **144**] sts).
Dec 1 st at each end of next 5 [**5**, 5, **7**, 7, **7**] rows, then on foll 10 [**11**, 12, **12**, 14, **15**] alt rows (80 [**84**, 88, **92**, 96, **100**] sts).
Cont straight until armhole meas 18 [**19**, 20, **21**, 23, **24**]cm (7 [**7¹/₂**, 8, **8¹/₂**, 9, **9¹/₂**]in), ending with RS facing for next row.
SHAPE SHOULDERS
Cast off 5 [**5**, 5, **6**, 6, **6**] sts at beg of next 6 [**4**, 2, **8**, 6, **4**] rows, then 6 [**6**, 6, **0**, 7, **7**] sts at beg of foll 2 [**4**, 6, **0**, 2, **4**] rows.
Leave rem 38 [**40**, 42, **44**, 46, **48**] sts on a holder.

Pocket linings (make 2)
With 3¹/₄mm (US 3) needles and MS, cast on 27 [**27**, 27, **31**, 31, **31**] sts.
Starting with a k row, work in stocking st for 11cm (4¹/₂in), ending with RS facing for next row.
Break yarn and leave sts on a holder.

Left front
With 2³/₄mm (US 2) needles and C, cast on 57 [**59**, 63, **67**, 71, **73**] sts.
Break off C and join in MS.
Work in rib as for Back for 5cm (2in), inc 1 st at centre of last row and ending with RS

facing for next row (58 [**60**, 64, **68**, 72, **74**] sts).
Change to 3¹/₄mm (US 3) needles.
Starting with a k row, cont in stocking st until
Left Front meas 16cm (6¹/₂in), ending with
RS facing for next row.**

PLACE POCKET
Next row (RS) K16 [**17**, 19, **19**, 21, **22**], slip
next 27 [**27**, 27, **31**, 31, **31**] sts onto a holder
and, in their place, k across 27 [**27**, 27, **31**,
31, **31**] sts of first Pocket Lining, k to end.
Cont straight until Left Front matches Back
to start of armhole shaping, ending with RS
facing for next row.

SHAPE ARMHOLE
Cast off 3 sts at beg of next row (55 [**57**, 61,
65, 69, **71**] sts).
Work 1 row.
Dec 1 st at armhole edge of next 5 [**5**, 5, **7**, 7,
7] rows, then on foll 10 [**11**, 12, **12**, 14, **15**] alt
rows (40 [**41**, 44, **46**, 48, **49**] sts).
Cont straight until 19 [**19**, 21, **21**, 23, **23**]
rows less have been worked than on Back to
start of shoulder shaping, ending with **WS**
facing for next row.

SHAPE NECK
Cast off 9 [**9**, 10, **11**, 12, **13**] sts at beg of next
row (31 [**32**, 34, **35**, 36, **36**] sts).
Dec 1 st at neck edge of next 10 [**10**, 11, **11**,
11, **10**] rows (21 [**22**, 23, **24**, 25, **26**] sts).
Work 8 [**8**, 9, **9**, 11, **12**] rows, ending with RS
facing for next row.

SHAPE SHOULDER
Cast off 5 [**5**, 5, **6**, 6, **6**] sts at beg of next and
foll 2 [**1**, 0, **2**, 2, **1**] alt rows, then 0 [**6**, 6, **0**, 0,
7] sts at beg of foll 0 [**1**, 2, **0**, 0, **1**] alt rows.
Work 1 row.
Cast off rem 6 [**6**, 6, **6**, 7, **7**] sts.

Right Front
Work as for Left Front to **.
PLACE POCKET
Next row (RS) K15 [**16**, 18, **18**, 20, **21**], slip

next 27 [**27**, 27, **31**, 31, **31**] sts onto a holder
and, in their place, k across 27 [**27**, 27, **31**,
31, **31**] sts of second Pocket Lining, k to end.
Complete to match Left Front, reversing
shapings, working an extra row before start
of armhole, neck and shoulder shaping.

Sleeves
With 2³/₄mm (US 2) needles and C, cast on 53
[**55**, 57, **57**, 59, **61**] sts.
Break off C and join in MS.
Work in rib as for Back for 5cm (2in), inc 1 st
at centre of last row and ending with RS
facing for next row (54 [**56**, 58, **58**, 60, **62**] sts).
Change to 3¹/₄mm (US 3) needles.
Starting with a k row, cont in stocking st,
shaping sides by inc 1 st at each end of 11th
[**9th**, next, **5th**, 5th, **5th**] and every foll 8th
row until there are 82 [**86**, 90, **80**, 76, **72**] sts.
91, 97 and 102cm (36, 38 and 40in)
sizes only:
Inc 1 st at each end of every foll 6th row until
there are [**92**, 96, **100**] sts.
All sizes:
Cont straight until Sleeve meas 42 [**42**, 43,
43, 43, **43**]cm (16¹/₂ [**16¹/₂**, 17, **17**, 17, **17**]in),
ending with RS facing for next row.
SHAPE TOP
Cast off 3 sts at beg of next 2 rows (76 [**80**,
84, **86**, 90, **94**] sts).
Dec 1 st at each end of next and foll 20 [**22**,
24, **27**, 29, **31**] alt rows, then on foll 3 [**3**, 3, **1**,
1, **1**] rows, ending with RS facing for next
row. Cast off rem 28 sts.

Make up
Press following instructions on ball band.
Join both shoulder seams.

Neck border
With RS facing, 2³/₄mm (US 2) needles and
MS, starting and ending at front opening

edges, **knit up** 22 [**23**, 24, **29**, 30, **31**] sts up right side of neck, k38 [**40**, 42, **44**, 46, **48**] from back inc 1 st at centre, then **knit up** 22 [**23**, 24, **29**, 30, **31**] sts down left side of neck (83 [**87**, 91, **103**, 107, **111**] sts).
Starting with rib row 2, work in rib as for Back for 10 rows, ending with **WS** facing for next row.
Break off MS and join in C.
Cast off in rib.

Button border
With 2³⁄₄mm (US 2) needles and C, cast on 11 sts.
Break off C and join in MS.
Row 1 (RS) K2, (p1, k1) 4 times, k1.
Row 2 K1, (p1, k1) 5 times.
Rep these 2 rows until Button Border, when slightly stretched, fits up left front opening edge to top of Neck Border, sewing in place as you go along and ending with **WS** facing for next row.
Break off MS and join in C.
Cast off in rib.
Mark positions for 9 buttons on this Border – first to come 1cm (³⁄₈in) up from cast-on edge, last to come in centre of Neck Border, and rem 7 buttons evenly spaced between.

Buttonhole border
Work to match Button Border, with the addition of 9 buttonholes worked to correspond with positions marked for buttons.
To make a buttonhole: On a RS row, rib 4, cast off 3 sts, rib to end; then rib back, casting on 3 sts over those cast off on previous row.

Pocket tops (both alike)
Slip 27 [**27**, 27, **31**, 31, **31**] sts from pocket holder onto 2³⁄₄mm (US 2) needles and

rejoin MS with RS facing.
Starting with rib row 1, work in rib as for Back for 2cm (³⁄₄in), ending with **WS** facing for next row.
Break off MS and join in C.
Cast off in rib.
Join side seams. Join sleeve seams. Insert Sleeves. Sew Pocket Linings in place on inside, then neatly sew down ends of Pocket Tops. Sew on buttons.

Boot socks

✪✪ *These classic long gumboot socks are knitted up in really warm Aran yarn, for great insulation on a cold winter's day. They are knitted on four double-pointed needles.*

You will need
- *Patons Diploma Gold Aran*:
    5 [**5**, 5] x 50g balls in grey (shade no. 08184) or off-white (shade no. 08121)
- Set of 4 double-pointed 4mm (US 6) knitting needles

Tension and finished size
- 20 stitches and 26 rows to 10cm (4in) over stocking stitch using 4mm (US 6) needles.
- Length of foot – 23 [**25**, 28]cm (9 [**10**, 11]in).
- Finished length – 38cm (15in).

Sock (make 2)
With double-pointed 4mm (US 6) needles, cast on 52 sts, distributing sts evenly over 3 needles (17 sts on first 2 needles and 18 sts on 3rd needle).
Round 1 (RS) *K2, p2; rep from * to end.
Rep this round for 10cm (4in), dec 1 st at end of last round (51 sts – 17 sts on each needle).
Proceed thus:
Round 1 (RS) K2tog, k to last 2 sts, k2tog tbl (49 sts).
Rounds 2 to 6 Knit.
Rounds 7 to 12 As rounds 1 to 6 (47 sts).
Round 13 As round 1 (45 sts).
Round 14 Knit.
Rep last round until work meas 30cm (12in).

SHAPE HEEL
Next round (RS) K11 and turn, slip last 12 sts of previous round onto other end of this needle (23 heel sts now on this needle), and then divide rem 22 instep sts between rem 2 needles.
Work on 23 heel sts only thus:
Next row (WS) SL1P, p22, turn.
Next row SL1K, k22, turn.
Rep last 2 rows 9 times more, then first of these rows again, ending with RS facing for next row.
Next row (RS) K13, sL1K, k1, psso, turn.
Next row P4, p2tog, turn.
Next row K5, sL1K, k1, psso, turn.
Next row P6, p2tog, turn.
Cont in this way until all heel sts are on one needle, ending with RS facing for next row.
Next row (RS) K7.
Heel complete.
Slip all 22 sts instep sts onto one needle.
With RS facing and using a spare needle, k rem 6 heel sts, **knit up** 15 sts along side of heel, using another needle k 22 instep sts, using another needle **knit up** 14 sts along other side of heel, then k other 7 heel sts (64 sts – 21 sts on first needle, 22 instep sts on second needle, and 21 sts on third needle).
Next round (RS) Knit.
Next round K to last 3 sts on first needle, k2tog, k1, k all 22 sts on second needle, work across sts on third needle thus: k1, k2tog tbl, k to end.
Rep last 2 rounds 9 times more (44 sts).
Next round (RS) Knit.
Rep last round until work meas 14 [**17**,

19]cm (5¹/₂ [**6¹/₂**, 7¹/₂]in) from knitted-up sts at heel.

SHAPE TOE

Next round (RS) K to last 3 sts on first needle, k2tog, k1, work across sts on second needle thus: k1, k2tog tbl, k to last 3 sts, k2tog, k1, work across sts on third needle thus: k1, k2tog tbl, k to end.

Next round Knit.

Rep last 2 rounds 4 times more (24 sts). Knit across sts on first needle, transferring them onto same needle as last set of sts. Arrange sts so that there are 2 sets of 12 sts on needles. Fold sock flat so that needles holding sts are next to each other and, using a third needle, cast off sts from both needles together to form toe seam.

Make up

Press following instructions on ball band.

Wool gloves

✪✪✪ *You will need to use four double-pointed needles for these gloves, as they are knitted so as to create a tubular seamless fabric. The yarn chosen is a wool mix, making them really warm for cold winter weather.*

You will need
- *Patons Diploma Gold DK:*
  2 [**2**] x 50g balls in **MS** – grey (shade no. 06184) or taupe (shade no. 06237)
  Small amount in **C** – green (shade no. 06125) or ginger (shade no. 06211)
- Set of 4 double-pointed 3¼mm (US 3) knitting needles

Tension and finished size
- 24 stitches and 32 rows to 10cm (4in) over stocking stitch using 3¼mm (US 3) needles.
- Width around hand – 17 [**20**]cm (6½ [**8**]in).
- Finished length – 25 [**29**]cm (10 [**11½**]in).

Right glove
With double-pointed 3¼mm (US 3) needles and C, cast on 38 [**44**] sts, distributing sts evenly over 3 needles (12 [**15**] sts on first 2 needles and 13 [**14**] sts on 3rd needle).
Break off C and join in MS.
Round 1 (RS) *K1, p1; rep from * to end.
Rep this round 21 [**23**] times more.
Next round (RS) (K11 [**13**], inc in next st) 3 times, k2 (41 [**47**] sts).**
SHAPE FOR THUMB
Rounds 1 and 2 K22 [**25**], p1, k3, p1, k14 [**17**].
Round 3 K22 [**25**], p1, inc once in each of next 2 sts, k1, p1, k14 [**17**] (43 [**49**] sts).

Rounds 4 and 5 K22 [**25**], p1, k5, p1, k14 [**17**].
Round 6 K22 [**25**], p1, inc in next st, k2, inc in next st, k1, p1, k14 [**17**] (45 [**51**] sts).
Rounds 7 and 8 K22 [**25**], p1, k7, p1, k14 [**17**].
Round 9 K22 [**25**], p1, inc in next st, k4, inc in next st, k1, p1, k14 [**17**] (47 [**53**] sts).
Rounds 10 and 11 K22 [**25**], p1, k9, p1, k14 [**17**].
Round 12 K22 [**25**], p1, inc in next st, k6, inc in next st, k1, p1, k14 [**17**] (49 [**55**] sts).
Rounds 13 and 14 K22 [**25**], p1, k11, p1, k14 [**17**].
Round 15 K22 [**25**], p1, inc in next st, k8, inc in next st, k1, p1, k14 [**17**] (51 [**57**] sts).
Rounds 16 and 17 K22 [**25**], p1, k13, p1, k14 [**17**].
Larger size only:
Round 18 K25, p1, inc in next st, k10, inc in next st, k1, p1, k17 (59 sts).
Rounds 19 and 20 K25, p1, k15, p1, k17.
Both sizes:
Next round K23 [**26**], slip next 15 sts onto a holder for thumb, cast on 4 sts, k to end (40 [**48**] sts).
Knit 13 [**16**] rounds.
SHAPE FIRST FINGER
Next round K12 [**15**] and slip these sts onto a holder, k12 [**14**], slip rem 16 [**19**] sts onto a holder, cast on 2 sts (14 [**16**] sts).
***Distribute these 14 [**16**] sts evenly over 3 needles and proceed thus:
Knit 21 [**25**] rounds.
Next round (K1, k2tog) 4 [**5**] times, k2 [**1**] (10 [**11**] sts).
Next round Knit.
Next round (K2tog) 5 times, k0 [**1**].

Break yarn and thread through rem 5 [**6**] sts.
Pull up tight and fasten off securely.

SHAPE SECOND FINGER

Next round (RS) Rejoin yarn and k next 5 [**6**] sts after first finger from holder, leave next 18 [**22**] sts on holder, cast on 2 sts, k rem 5 [**6**] sts on holder, then **knit up** 2 sts from base of first finger (14 [**16**] sts).
Distribute these 14 [**16**] sts evenly over 3 needles and proceed thus:
Knit 23 [**27**] rounds.
Next round (K1, k2tog) 4 [**5**] times, k2 [**1**] (10 [**11**] sts).
Next round Knit.
Next round (K2tog) 5 times, k0 [**1**].
Break yarn and thread through rem 5 [**6**] sts.
Pull up tight and fasten off securely.

SHAPE THIRD FINGER

Next round (RS) Rejoin yarn and k next 5 [**6**] sts after second finger from holder, leave next 8 [**10**] sts on holder, cast on 2 sts, k rem 5 [**6**] sts on holder, then **knit up** 2 sts from base of second finger (14 [**16**] sts).
Distribute these 14 [**16**] sts evenly over 3 needles and proceed thus:
Knit 21 [**25**] rounds.
Next round (K1, k2tog) 4 [**5**] times, k2 [**1**] (10 [**11**] sts).
Next round Knit.
Next round (K2tog) 5 times, k0 [**1**].
Break yarn and thread through rem 5 [**6**] sts.
Pull up tight and fasten off securely.

SHAPE FOURTH FINGER

Next round Rejoin yarn and k 8 [**10**] sts on holder, then **knit up** 2 sts from base of third finger (10 [**12**] sts).
Distribute these 10 [**12**] sts evenly over 3 needles and proceed thus:
Knit 17 [**21**] rounds.
Next round (K1, k2tog) 3 [**4**] times, k1 [**0**] (7 [**8**] sts).
Next round Knit.

Next round (K2tog) 3 [**4**] times, k1 [**0**].
Break yarn and thread through rem 4 sts.
Pull up tight and fasten off securely.

SHAPE THUMB

Next round Rejoin yarn and k 15 sts on thumb holder, then **knit up** 4 sts from base of hand section (19 sts).
Distribute these 19 sts evenly over 3 needles and proceed thus:
Knit 20 rounds.
Next round (K1, k2tog) 6 times, k1 (13 sts).
Next round Knit.
Next round K1, (k2tog) 6 times.
Break yarn and thread through rem 7 sts.
Pull up tight and fasten off securely.

Left glove

Work as for Right Glove to **.

SHAPE FOR THUMB

Rounds 1 and 2 K14 [**17**], p1, k3, p1, k22 [**25**].
Round 3 K14 [**17**], p1, inc once in each of next 2 sts, k1, p1, k22 [**25**] (43 [**49**] sts).
Rounds 4 and 5 K14 [**17**], p1, k5, p1, k22 [**25**].
Round 6 K14 [**17**], p1, inc in next st, k2, inc in next st, k1, p1, k22 [**25**] (45 [**51**] sts).
Rounds 7 and 8 K14 [**17**], p1, k7, p1, k22 [**25**].
Round 9 K14 [**17**], p1, inc in next st, k4, inc in next st, k1, p1, k22 [**25**] (47 [**53**] sts).
Rounds 10 and 11 K14 [**17**], p1, k9, p1, k22 [**25**].
Round 12 K14 [**17**], p1, inc in next st, k6, inc in next st, k1, p1, k22 [**25**] (49 [**55**] sts).
Rounds 13 and 14 K14 [**17**], p1, k11, p1, k22 [**25**].
Round 15 K14 [**17**], p1, inc in next st, k8, inc in next st, k1, p1, k22 [**25**] (51 [**57**] sts).
Rounds 16 and 17 K14 [**17**], p1, k13, p1, k22 [**25**].
Larger size only:
Round 18 K17, p1, inc in next st, k10, inc in next st, k1, p1, k25 (59 sts).
Rounds 19 and 20 K17, p1, k15, p1, k25.

Both sizes:
Next round K15 [**18**], slip next 15 sts onto a holder for thumb, cast on 4 sts, k to end (40 [**48**] sts).
Knit 13 [**16**] rounds.
SHAPE FIRST FINGER
Next round K19 [**22**] and slip these sts onto a holder, k12 [**14**], slip rem 9 [**12**] sts onto a holder, cast on 2 sts (14 [**16**] sts).

Complete Left Glove as for Right Glove from ***.

Make up
Press following instructions on ball band.

Knitting abbreviations

The following are the knitting abbreviations used in this book, plus some extra commonly used ones. Special abbreviations are always given within the pattern.

alt	alternate
approx	approximately
beg	begin(s)(ning)
C	contrasting shade of yarn
cm	centimetre(s)
cn	cable needle
cont	continu(e)(ing)
dec	decreas(e)(ing)
foll	follow(s)(ing)
g	gram(s)
g st	garter stitch (k every row)
in	inch(es)
inc	increase(e)(ing); in row instructions k (or p) into front and back of st to increase one
k	knit
knit up	pick up and knit stitches along edge of knitting
M1	make one stitch by picking up horizontal loop before next stitch and knitting into back of it
M1P	make one stitch by picking up horizontal loop before next stitch and purling into back of it
meas	measure(s)
mm	millimetres
MS	main shade of yarn
oz	ounce(s)
p	purl
patt	pattern; or, work in the pattern st
psso	pass slipped stitch over
p2sso	pass 2 slipped stitches over
rem	remain(s)(ing)
rep	repeat(s)(ing)
rev st st	reverse stocking stitch (p RS rows, k WS rows)
RS	right side
sl 1	slip one stitch
sL1K	slip next st knitways
sL1P	slip next st purlways
st(s)	stitch(es)
st st	stocking stitch (k RS rows, p WS rows)
tbl	through back of loop
tog	together
WS	wrong side
yd	yard(s)
yfwd	yarn forward
yfrn	yarn forward round needle
yon	yarn over needle

Sizes in patterns

In patterns that have a choice of sizes, the smallest size comes first and the remaining sizes follow inside square brackets [ ]. Where there is only one set of figures, it applies to all sizes. Be sure to follow the same size throughout the pattern.

Yarn information

For the best results, use the yarn specified for a particular pattern. If you cannot obtain the specified yarn, use the yarn specifications below to help obtain a similar substitute. Always calculate how much yarn you need by metrage/yardage rather than weight.

Yarn specifications and care

The following yarns were used for the projects in this book. A recommended knitting tension is given as a guide to yarn thickness. Always check the yarn label for care instructions before pressing or cleaning your knitting.

PATONS DIPLOMA GOLD 4 PLY
- Wool-mix, lightweight yarn.
- 55 per cent wool, 25 per cent acrylic and 20 per cent nylon.
- 50g ball (approximately 184m/201yd).
- 28 stitches and 36 rows to 10cm (4in) measured over stocking stitch using 3¼mm (US size 3) needles.

PATONS DIPLOMA GOLD DK
- Wool-mix, double-knitting weight yarn.
- 55 per cent wool, 25 per cent acrylic and 20 per cent nylon.
- 50g ball (approximately 120m/131yd).
- 22 stitches and 30 rows to 10cm (4in) measured over stocking stitch using 4mm (US size 6) needles.

PATONS DIPLOMA GOLD ARAN
- Wool-mix, Aran-weight yarn.
- 55 per cent wool, 25 per cent acrylic and 20 per cent nylon.

- 100g ball (approximately 164m/180yd).
- 19 stitches and 25 rows to 10cm (4in) measured over stocking stitch using 4½mm (US size 7) needles.

PATONS 100% COTTON 4 PLY
- Lightweight cotton yarn.
- 100 per cent cotton.
- 100g (approximately 210m/230yd).
- 28 stitches and 36 rows to 10cm (4in) measured over stocking stitch using 3¼mm (US size 3) needles.

Where to obtain yarns

The yarns and products featured in this book can be obtained from Coats Crafts UK. For further information, and to obtain lists of stockists both in the UK and overseas, visit the Coats website (www.coatscrafts.co.uk) or get in touch with them at
Coats Crafts UK
Lingfield Point
McMullen Road
Darlington
Co. Durham
DL1 1YQ
Tel +44 (0) 1325 394394

Acknowledgments

The publishers would like to thank the following people for their help with this book: Hilary Jagger for helping to select the yarn colours and patterns; Sue Whiting for pattern writing and checking; Stella Smith for pattern checking; Elizabeth Tunnicliffe for supplying yarns; Sally Harding for editing and proof-reading; Anne Wilson for the design; John Heseltine for the photography; Kate Simunek for the artwork; and Jayne Emerson and Edward Berry for modelling garments.